£2.00

THE DEVIL'S ACCOUNT

Also by Hugh Rayment-Pickard

The Myths of Time

Impossible God: Derrida's Theology

Philosophies of History from Enlightenment to Postmodernity
(with Robert Burns)

THE
DEVIL'S ACCOUNT

Philip Pullman and Christianity

HUGH RAYMENT-PICKARD

The Devil's account is, that the Messiah fell,
& formed a heaven of what he stole from the
* Abyss.*
(Blake, 'The Marriage of Heaven and Hell')

DARTON · LONGMAN + TODD

First published in 2004 by
Darton, Longman and Todd Ltd
1 Spencer Court
140–142 Wandsworth High Street
London
SW18 4JJ

ISBN 0 232 52563 3

A catalogue record for this book is available from the British Library.

Printed and bound in Great Britain by
Cromwell Press Ltd, Trowbridge, Wiltshire

For Ann and Martin,
my parents

CONTENTS

PREFACE

I am grateful to my wife Liz who first suggested that I should set aside my usual diet of philosophical books to read Pullman's *His Dark Materials* trilogy. The idea of a book about Pullman's religious ideas came from Rachel Davis at Darton, Longman and Todd and I benefited from Rachel's helpful criticism of the text. Rachel Carr and Alan Everett kindly read and re-read much of the material and, as ever, made extremely telling comments. I am also grateful to pupils from Blundells School who spent time talking with me about their reactions to Pullman's writing.

LIST OF ABBREVIATIONS

Quotations from Pullman's novels are referenced within parentheses in the text using the following abbreviations:

AS   *The Amber Spyglass* (Scholastic, 2000)
BB   *The Broken Bridge* (Macmillan, 2001)
BT   *The Butterfly Tattoo* (Macmillan, 2001)
Gal   *Galatea* (E. P. Dutton, 1979)
HS   *The Haunted Storm* (New English Library, 1972)
NL   *Northern Lights* (Scholastic, 1998)
RS   *The Ruby in the Smoke* (Scholastic, 1999)
SK   *The Subtle Knife* (Scholastic, 1998)
SN   *The Shadow in the North* (Scholastic, 1999)
TP   *The Tin Princess* (Scholastic, 2000)
TW   *The Tiger in the Well* (Scholastic, 1999)

PART ONE

Introduction

The religious atheist

> *Student:* I'm an atheist!
> *G. K. Chesterton:* I envy you your simple faith.

I am one of Philip Pullman's most enthusiastic and dedicated readers. When I read *His Dark Materials* for the first time, I consumed all three books in almost as many days. Since then I have read them all again twice. But I didn't just *enjoy* these books, I was *intrigued* by Pullman's atheism – an atheism that seemed to me to be so thoroughly *religious*. I had the feeling that Philip Pullman, like many enthusiastic non-believers, was still secretly in love with both theology and the theological enchantment of the world. I wanted to explore the strange underlying paradox of what I am calling Pullman's 'religious atheism'.

After reading the trilogy, I went on to read all of Pullman's adult and teenage fiction. These books are very varied – ranging from magical–realist novels (fashionable in the 1970s) to detective stories and issue-driven 'teen' fiction dealing with race, feminism, adoption and child abuse. Pullman is certainly versatile, but in every book I kept tripping over religious themes: strange priests, diabolical evil, religious searchers, explorations of the real and the unreal, good and evil, spirit and matter, God and the devil, and ideas about ultimate human meaning and destiny. I became even more curious about the nature of Pullman's religious concerns: was he simply hostile to religion, or was there perhaps a religious quest hidden somewhere within his antagonism?

I don't mean to suggest that Pullman is not sincere. He is a passionate and unapologetic atheist, who has no time for the church. But the mystery is: why does he devote so much energy to religious and theological topics? Perhaps the religious questions are important to Pullman, even if he doesn't like the Christian answers.

One upshot of Pullman's 'religious atheism' is that his fiction contains an inner tension between the novelist and the philosopher, between the story-teller and the anti-theologian. As we will see, Pullman is convinced in his own mind that he is just a teller of stories. This in itself is strange, because if there is one thing that can be confidently said of Pullman the novelist, it is that he *never* just writes stories. There is always something more: some message or meaning.

This book is an attempt to explore and understand what Pullman's message is. What is going on – theologically speaking – in his fiction? How does Pullman use his fiction to explore theological issues? What does Pullman mean by story-telling, and what do his stories actually tell us? What is Pullman's case against religion and what are his own religious concerns?

Everyone likes straightforward answers to straightforward questions. But given the paradoxes at the heart of Pullman's writing, straightforward answers may not be forthcoming. Pullman's writing may be the kind that supplies more questions than answers.

Pullman's writing before *His Dark Materials*

Pullman's career as a writer began with an adult novel, *The Haunted Storm* (1972). Pullman does not talk about this book except to describe it as 'a load of crap'.[1] Pullman is too harsh, although *The Haunted Storm* is not a great novel. Lady Antonia Fraser gave the novel an endorsement as 'an honest and enterprising attempt to interweave the eternal – and immortal – longings of youth into the texture of a contemporary story'.[2] *The Haunted Storm* is certainly a serious book that reveals the scale of Pullman's literary ambition. The hero refers on one occasion to Dostoyevsky's *The Brothers Karamazov*, and this is the kind of example that Pullman would like to follow: the exploration of fundamental theological and ethical issues. We also see in this book how Pullman likes to take up controversial and transgressive sexual and ethical themes which reappear in his later writing, particularly in *Galatea* (see pp. 27–29 below) and *The Butterfly Tattoo*.

The Haunted Storm is a quasi-religious novel about different kinds of searches for ultimate meaning and security, symbolised in the novel by a mysterious Holy Well, whose significance is unclear. Matthew (the hero) is an edgy searcher, looking for meaning in an array of theologies and philosophies, and his visit to the Well results in his enlightenment. Alan (his satanic brother) is trying to pass the Well off as a pagan symbol of 'the invincible god' in order to promote his vicious fascist politics. The Revd Cole (a Gnostic vicar) sees the Well as a source of goodness in a world shrouded in darkness and corruption. Elizabeth (the hero's girlfriend and the vicar's daughter) is looking for meaning through her relationships with men, and in the end finds them all lacking. The four main characters are contrasted with

Harry (the hero's uncle), who has an unshakeable Christian faith in the goodness of God. The novel – like many examples of philosophical fiction – is structured around set-piece conversations in which ideas are exchanged and debated.

Although the novel is a rather confused and unsuccessful attempt to open up a range of sexual, psychological, ethical and religious themes, it does reveal very clearly Pullman's interest in theology. The hero believes in God, but is troubled by God's apparent absence in the material processes of the world, symbolised by 'the storm'. The hero's experiences lead him to the Nietzschean conclusion that the world is 'perspectival': so contradictory views – such as his uncle's and the vicar's – can simultaneously be correct. He realises that there is no hidden depth to the world: 'Things existed: that was it, that was all that could be said: things existed' (HS 235). The hero finds the conviction that he and the world 'are one and the same thing' and that he must create the meaning of his own life, rather than waiting for some revelation. It turns out in the end that the Well is dedicated to 'the unknown god' rather than 'the invincible god'. So the novel ends on an agnostic rather than an atheistic cadence, leaving room for some possible unknown god to appear.

The Haunted Storm shows Pullman's appetite for telling stories that deal with 'big ideas'. The maturation of these big ideas takes place over the 25 years between *The Haunted Storm* and *His Dark Materials*, which is not only an adventure story, but a narrative statement about what Douglas Adams called 'life, the universe and everything'.

The Haunted Storm was followed by another adult novel, *Galatea* (1978), which Pullman still regards with affection. *Galatea* – as we will see later – explores a number of themes that re-surface in *His Dark Materials*. The hero chases after his missing wife though a magical–realist dimension of fantastic cities. One of these cities, like Lyra's world in *His Dark Materials*, is an evil theocracy.

Pullman's most important children's fiction before *His Dark Materials* is a quartet of novels based on the adventures of Sally Lockhart and her friends: *The Ruby in the Smoke* (1985); *The Shadow in the North* (1986); *The Tiger in the Well* (1991) and *The Tin Princess* (1994). At the time, these stories must have seemed simply to be accomplished novels of high adventure. In retrospect we can see Pullman experimenting with many of the themes of his later trilogy. The heroine is a plucky young woman, Sally Lockhart, who takes on diabolical enemies. Like Lyra, Sally is fired by personal confidence and basic values of loyalty, courage and honesty.

In the Sally Lockhart novels we see Pullman's interest in ultimate evil and the forces that are required to combat it. Sally's arch-enemy (in *The Ruby in the Smoke* and *The Tiger in the Well*) is Ah Ling, who functions as Pullman's Satan, Moriarty or Fu Manchu: an exemplary enemy who must not only be stopped but *destroyed*. Ah Ling is not a mere criminal who needs punishing or restraining: he represents an absolute evil that must be overcome absolutely. Ah Ling uses many names, including 'Todd' (presumably Sweeney Todd), to indicate his extreme violence and cruelty. He is a polymorphous villain, 'a mysterious figure' (TW 24) who speaks 'without trace of any accent' (RS 193). 'No one usually sees him because he always travels at night' (TW 26) and he is known only by rumour and folklore. He is the descendant of Chinese pirates, educated in Europe, but operating in Warsaw, Bucharest and London; and he is accompanied by 'a little imp from hell', a small monkey who waits on his every need. Ah Ling, who has agents all over Europe, is also behind a 'conspiracy, organisation, plot, whatever' to persecute the Jews (TW 199).

Ah Ling is contrasted unfavourably with the equally dastardly Axel Bellman, the villain of *The Shadow in the North*. Bellman's crime is the construction of a massive machine gun that can be used by governments to subdue civil unrest. Bellman is a vile character, but Sally explains that he is at least motivated (however perversely) by the noble aim of keeping law and order. But Bellman does not represent the wickedness of society or capitalism or anything else. Bellman's scheme must be destroyed, but Bellman's death is not a moral necessity in the way that Ah Ling's is. Bellman reeks of power and its misuse, but not of evil. Bellman is 'wrong' says Sally because he doesn't understand 'loyalty', 'love' or 'people' (SN 274).

Ah Ling dies for more primitive moral reasons. Just before he dies, Sally takes the opportunity to deliver a speech to Ah Ling on the nature of an evil that contaminates all humanity.

> Listen to me and learn. Evil . . . It's what makes a family starve . . . And do you know what's at the heart of it all? Eh? The gnawing poison cancer destroying and eating and laying waste at the heart of it all? It's not only you, you poor pitiful man; it's *me* too. Me and ten thousand others . . . I didn't know the consequences of things . . . We are all connected. (TW 338)

Although he is not personally responsible for all the wickedness in the world, Ah Ling, and his vicious monkey, *symbolise* the evil of the world in which Sally too is implicated – and for that reason he cannot survive.

Just as the dæmons of *His Dark Materials* represent the

8

souls of the characters in Lyra's universe, so Ah Ling's monkey symbolises his heart of darkness:

> 'It's evil', said Rebecca, as she rubbed something pungent into Sally's hair. 'I don't care what they say about animals being innocent, not knowing good or evil, Adam and Eve, the Tree of Knowledge, blah, blah – that monkey is not innocent. It knows evil and it does evil. If I believed in all that folklore stuff about dybbuks and golems and so on, I'd think it was an evil spirit, not an animal of flesh and blood.' (TW 250)

In fact Ah Ling is not killed by Sally (who has already failed to polish him off with a point-blank pistol shot in *The Ruby in the Smoke*) but by a flood that also wipes out his henchmen and, symbolically, sweeps away his entire house. It is a gothic, apocalyptic death that smacks of final judgement. Ah Ling is not subjected to mere human justice but is destroyed by a cosmic force that intervenes to show that history is ultimately on the side of the good.

Ah Ling is also known by the ironic title 'Ttzaddik' which means 'religious one, saint, holy man' (TW 26). This is a hint of what is to come in *His Dark Materials*, where the evil to be overcome is God himself. Ah Ling is given a divine name 'as a way of keeping evil at bay' (TW 26). The religious themes are not developed at all in the Lockhart stories, but Pullman is already suggesting that there might be some coincidence between divinity and evil. Of course, if God is evil, then he too must be swept away. And so the logic of an enemy who *must* be destroyed is repeated in *His Dark Materials*, but this time the enemy is the Authority (God). Lord Asriel's servant Thorold explains to Serafina Pekkala that his master's ambition is not to defeat the church because that would leave the source of the church's power intact. Asriel is 'a-going to find the Authority and kill Him' (SK 48) and this *destruction*, as we learn, is an absolute requirement for the future growth of humanity. In the end, the Authority is revealed as a feeble old man 'crying like a baby', just as Ah Ling is shown as a pathetic figure, paralysed by Sally's gunshot and driven by the petty motives of greed and revenge.

The theme of radical evil is explored in a more direct and theological way in *The Butterfly Tattoo* (1992, also called *The White Mercedes*). Chris, the hero of the novel, is tempted by the evil Carson who has an inhuman face 'illuminated like hell fire' (BT 180). Of himself, Carson says 'I'm a demon, me. I'm a killer. I'm the angel of death' (BT 181). Carson offers Chris a revised version of the Genesis temptation story (for more on this see pp. 70–72 below), arguing that experience is preferable to innocence. But in contrast to *His Dark Materials* or the Lockhart novels, Pullman allows evil to win. Chris's girl-friend is shot dead – with Chris's collusion – and the novel ends not only with Carson going free, but with his dark ideology unanswered. *The Butterfly Tattoo* is Pullman at his very best: ambivalent, morally complex and unsettling.

The religious reception of *His Dark Materials*

Looking back at the reviews of the trilogy, we see that *His Dark Materials* has drawn both the highest praise and the most scathing criticism. Readers seem either to love Pullman's trilogy or hate it, but few are indifferent or lukewarm in their reactions. The reason for this is that most readers recognised Pullman's anti-Christian agenda and either warmed to it or wanted to warn against it.

Nick Thorpe, writing in *The Sunday Times*, described Pullman as an 'anti-Christian fundamentalist', and a writer in the *Guardian* called him 'an evangelical atheist'. Whatever reviewers have said about Pullman's writing – and Pullman's story-telling gifts have generally been applauded, even by those who dislike his message – it is Pullman's big ideas that have attracted the most attention.

Predictably, readers from the conservative Christian right found the trilogy offensive. Peter Hitchens, writing in the *Mail on Sunday*, saw Pullman as an atheist messiah: 'He is . . . the one the atheists would have been praying for, if atheists prayed.' ('The Most Dangerous Man in Britain'). Hitchens found *His Dark Materials* 'too loaded down with propaganda to leave enough room for the story'. The *Catholic Herald* claimed his work was 'the stuff of nightmares', and a writer from the Association of Christian Teachers said that Pullman was shamelessly blasphemous and had 'wilfully set out to exploit children in order to advance his own atheistic agenda'. At the fundamentalist extreme, internet sites in the US have called Pullman 'satanic'.

More subtle and insightful commentators have noted Pullman's positive religious concerns. John Pridmore, writing in the *Church Times*, said that Pullman's trilogy would be the inspiration for numerous Church of England sermons. Andrew Marr, writing in the *Daily Telegraph*, made a similar point from a secular perspective:

> What he gives me and what excites me is the sense that a post-Christian world can be as intensely filled with pity, the search for goodness, and an acute awareness of evil, as any religious universe.[3]

Rowan Williams, among others, has also noted Pullman's religious relevance. It is this 'relevance' that has intrigued me: how is Pullman's writing *relevant* to religious concerns when he is, apparently, so utterly hostile to any religious system? Why does Pullman attract religious interest, when he never claims to be setting out religious ideas at all? He is, if he is to be believed, just a teller of stories.

PART TWO

The Story-teller

'A contest of imaginations' (Gal 160)

Philip Pullman was born on 19 October 1946. The young Pullman grew up in an age in which serious children's fiction was dominated by two giants: J. R. R. Tolkien and C. S. Lewis. In 1949 Tolkien completed *The Lord of the Rings*. In 1950 C. S. Lewis published *The Lion, the Witch and the Wardrobe* and the remaining six parts of *The Chronicles of Narnia* appeared over the following five years.

Tolkien believed that Christian truths were best expressed in stories, principally the narrative of the gospel, which he saw as 'the greatest story of all'. He felt that the language of doctrine was too restricted and thin to gather up the rich and complex truth of Christianity. So Tolkien committed himself to *mythopoesis*: the construction of new myths to re-express the essence of the Christian message. C. S. Lewis, Tolkien's friend, tried to distil the same message into an epic metaphysical adventure story for children. Both Tolkien and Lewis attempted to express the Christian worldview through strange mythical universes: Middle-Earth and Narnia.

Fifty years later the adult Pullman would also reach the conclusion that the truth is best communicated in myth and story. But Pullman's *mythopoesis* would have a different purpose: not the defence of Christian truth, but its destruction. Pullman would show his readers a world in which God dies and in which religious organisations, practices and beliefs are violent and malevolent. Indeed Pullman would write his myth precisely to combat the Christian myths of Lewis and Tolkien.

This is a strange form of combat: neither a battle of rational arguments which would prove Christianity right or wrong, nor a contest of authorities or revelations. Pullman engages in a contest of *narratives*: he tries to 'out-narrate' Christianity, to tell a better story. Pullman tries to win readers with a myth that is simply more appealing, more powerful, and more convincing than the Christian narrative. It is clear from Pullman's book sales and literary awards that his myth has met with some considerable success in its battle with the Christian story.

Pullman offers the poet's (rather than the philosopher's) rejoinder to Christianity. It is not Christian *ideas* that offend Pullman so much as the Christian *myth*. When, for example, Pullman criticises C. S. Lewis, it is not the theology *per se* that offends him, but Lewis' failures, cruelties and irresponsibilities as a story-teller. Pullman believes that the Christian story diminishes humanity and that it must be replaced with a new myth of human dignity.

In his novels Pullman often dramatises the strategic use of stories. In *Northern Lights*, the heroine Lyra outwits Iofur Raknison by telling a crafty story. Later she releases the lost souls from hell by soothing the harpies with tales from her life. In *The Tiger in the Well* Danny Goldberg (Sally's future husband) holds back a rioting crowd by telling them stories:

> What a lucky bugger I am, he said to himself.
> Talk for your life, Danny boy. Tell 'em a story.
> 'I need a chair,' he said loudly . . . They

didn't know what to make of it, but in the face of his brazen confidence they felt their anger tremble a little, uncertainly. (TW 347–8)

Goldberg stills the crowd by identifying the many stories of oppression that lie behind their discontent. 'Goldberg knew that the people are hungry to have their own experience voiced; he was saying all this for them' (TW 349). Here and elsewhere, Pullman casts the story-teller in heroic terms. The story-teller's task is not merely to entertain, but to challenge, resist and liberate. Stories are an ideological force, an instrument of truth. Pullman sees himself as like Danny Goldberg: the lone story-teller standing on a chair before the crowds of religious unreason, superstition and authoritarian oppression.

Pullman's childhood prepared him very well for the task of challenging the Christian myth. After his father died in an air crash, Pullman spent a period in Norfolk with his maternal grandfather, who was a Church of England parson. It was from his grandfather that Pullman learned the stories in the Bible and the languages of the Authorised Version, the Book of Common Prayer and *Hymns Ancient and Modern*. Pullman was immersed in Anglican culture, attending church and Sunday school and becoming confirmed. He has said that the linguistic riches of the Anglican tradition have formed 'a deep and inescapable part of [his] nature'[1] and Pullman is, consequently, rather stuffy about 'the dreadful, barren language that disfigures the forms of services they have now'.[2]

Despite (or perhaps because of) his Anglican upbringing, Pullman found it impossible to believe. Religious language may have been a powerful influence, but Pullman could find 'no sign of God – a living God':

> So I have to consider myself an atheist. But because of my upbringing I'm a Christian atheist, and I'm a church atheist . . . I'm a 1662 Book of Common Prayer atheist, a *Hymns Ancient and Modern* atheist, a King James Bible atheist.[3]

It is not surprising, then, that Pullman was attracted to more literary and experimental treatments of the Christian tradition – in particular those of Milton and Blake. Pullman was already deeply impressed by Milton before going to read English at Oxford in the late 1960s. Milton and Blake not only impressed Pullman with their grand style, but with their mythic imagination. Both poets were playing with the possibilities and variations of the Christian myth, just as Pullman would in his trilogy. Many of the chapters in *The Amber Spyglass* start, self-consciously, with quotations from Blake, Milton and the Bible.

Although Milton's aim was to defend the Christian myth, he inadvertently glamorised evil and transgression. Milton's expressed purpose in *Paradise Lost* was to 'justify the ways of God to Man' by retelling the story of the Fall. But the most interesting and appealing of Milton's characters is Satan, and the reader finds him/herself in sympathy with Satan. Milton made Satan appear like one of us, not attractive but at least human in his thoughts and feelings. For this reason, Blake said that Milton 'was of the Devil's party without knowing it'. Pullman has said that he sees himself 'of the Devil's party, but I know it.'[4]

Blake's mythology is altogether more complicated and difficult to interpret. Blake saw Jesus as the embodiment of every virtue, but despised God the Father ('Urizen' in his mythology) as a tyrant and oppressor. Blake saw the 'authority' of God as an obstacle to human freedom and life-expression, and disliked churches because they denied the life-giving message of Jesus, and separated religion from ordinary natural life. In the spirit of Blake, Pullman calls God 'the Authority'. Pullman also shares Blake's anti-clericalism and suspicion of organised religion.

Pullman resembles Blake in another way: like Blake he must *use* and therefore advertise the Christian myth in order to *subvert* it. St Paul said that there can be no transgression without law (Romans 4:15). A corollary to that is: *transgression reminds us that there is law*. In order to attack religion, Pullman ends up telling a religious story. For example, Pullman's heroine Lyra descends to the land of the dead to rescue its lost souls. This is a conscious echo of Jesus' descent into Hell and there are many such parallels in *His Dark Materials*. In a strange way Pullman's counter-myth may help to keep the Christian myth alive, because it is not possible to understand *His Dark Materials* without also understanding the power and appeal of the Christian story. Like all artistic transgressors, Pullman pays homage to the sacred power that he seeks to overcome.

The implicit paradox behind any artistic transgression of the sacred is this: the very act of transgression is an acknowledgement of the power and status of the transgressed object. Don Cupitt comments on this in respect of Andreas Serrano's image *Piss Christ*, a crucifix immersed in the artist's urine. 'When we look at Serrano's *Piss Christ*, we should ask ourselves: which strikes us as being the stronger power – the holiness of the crucifix or the uncleanness of the urine?'[5] In a strange way, sacrilege actually *affirms* the sacred. As one of Pullman's own characters puts it:

'It seems impossible, that grossness, but it's
sanctified, obscenity is blessed by it. In fact
the more obscene the more holy the result, if
you are dealing in holiness, or the lovelier, if
you are dealing in beauty.' (Gal 129)

As an example of transgression, Pullman's *His Dark
Materials* is pretty tame, at least when compared say to
Serrano's work, or Gilbert and George's *Shit Faith*, or Jeff
Koons' pornographic images of heaven. But if we look at
his earlier adult fiction, we discover that Pullman is
every bit as bold in his transgression as Serrano, Koons
or Gilbert and George. In *Galatea*, for example, the hero
has anal sex with an angel and sin is likened to a mountain full of excrement. In *The Haunted Storm* the hero
masturbates a complete stranger as she discusses her personal problems. Pullman is a transgressive writer who
deliberately tries to test the boundaries between the
sacred and the profane and between good and bad taste.

Pullman's transgressive gestures, like all others, also
play to the advantage of the sacred. Despite itself, *His
Dark Materials* is in fact a positive resource for those who
want to understand the Christian myth. Archbishop
Rowan Williams has suggested that Pullman's trilogy
should go on the national religious education curricu-
lum. The Scripture Union has brought out a Bible study
guide to *His Dark Materials*, believing that Pullman's
writing will help Christians to 'dig into their Bibles, and
get to know them better'.[6] Pullman's book does not so
much dispose of religious concern, as *provoke* it. Despite
its strong anti-Christian polemic, Pullman's trilogy may
yet be remembered as a valuable contribution to
Christian debate.

The teller and the tale

The question of how and why we tell stories is at the centre of Pullman's understanding of his writing. Pullman speaks frequently – within his fiction and elsewhere – about the story-telling imperative, about the ethics of story-telling, and about the centrality of stories not only to human culture, but to the identity of the human species: 'Stories are the most important things in the world,' says Pullman, 'without stories, we wouldn't be human beings at all.' Pullman sees himself not so much as a 'writer' as a teller of stories.

> I tell a story. I see myself as being in an old-fashioned kind of market-place – a little country town if you like – where people are buying and selling food; and farmers coming in; people buying grain and eating and drinking and gossiping and talking; and maybe over there, a fellow with a violin playing a tune or fiddle; and here's a juggler juggling some things; and maybe there's a pickpocket over there doing something he shouldn't be doing. And here am I sitting in the middle of all this busy activity on my little bit of carpet telling a story.[7]

There is something attractive, understated and humble about this portrait of the artist. Pullman is not making any claims about 'literature' or 'art'. He is just a teller of tales.

Story is so important to Pullman that he says that he would like to 'disappear' behind his stories and become 'invisible'. The story is what matters and not the personality.[8] Despite his attempts to vanish behind his stories, Pullman is certainly no recluse like J. D. Salinger or

Thomas Pynchon. He is a prolific interviewee, speaker and essayist. Indeed few writers have ever had such a visible public profile. And Pullman's own views on Christianity, C. S. Lewis and the uses of literature have been expressed powerfully and frequently in the media. Pullman is an international celebrity and the story of Philip Pullman attracts nearly as much attention as the stories he writes.

When Pullman says that he would like to 'disappear' behind his story, he presumably means that he does not want his own personality and attitudes to be an issue *in the text*. He would like the stories to stand alone as self-contained fictions, creations in their own right that do not require an understanding of the author and his views. If this is the case, Pullman has surely not succeeded in disappearing. His views about Christianity in particular are as well known as his novels. When I told people that I was writing about Pullman, they were as likely to say 'you mean the guy who thinks God is dead' as 'you mean the guy who wrote *His Dark Materials*'. Pullman's aim to be the story-teller in the market-place has been frustrated by the widespread assumption that his novels are more than stories, and that they contain controversial views about God and religion.

Despite the powerful public perception that his books contain more than just good stories, Pullman strongly denies that he has any 'message' for his readers:

> The aim was always to tell the story. But you don't set out to preach, you don't set out to persuade or to give a lecture or to teach, heaven forbid, don't set out to teach. You just set out to entertain, to tell a story.[9]

It's a story, not a treatise, not a sermon or a work of philosophy. I'm telling a story, I'm showing various characters whom I've invented saying things and doing things and acting out beliefs which they have, and not necessarily which I have. The tendency of the whole thing might be this or it might be that, but what I'm doing is telling a story, not preaching a sermon.[10]

I believe that Pullman is sincere when he says these things, but he is surely out of touch with the ideological and pedagogical voice which resounds so clearly through *His Dark Materials*. It is very strange that a voice so audible to his readers cannot be heard by Pullman himself.

There is a massive tension between Pullman's self-perception and the persona he projects in his fiction. Pullman sees himself as the humble story-teller, but his novels show him to be someone who wants to communicate a powerful and strongly-held ideology. From within the story, Pullman is trying to instruct us about religion and the meaning of life.

'The story made me do it'

At the end of *The Amber Spyglass* the two main characters Will and Lyra decide to sacrifice their love for each other in order to fulfil their higher spiritual destiny. Will must return to his world, and smash the magical knife that has enabled him to travel between parallel universes. Lyra must return to her world and begin the task of building the republic of heaven. Love must give way to duty, pleasure to responsibility.

Having built up the relationship between his main

characters, Pullman has to destroy it. He admits that he found the decision difficult: 'I tried all sorts of ways to prevent it, but the story made me do it. That was what had to happen. If I'd denied it, the story wouldn't have had a tenth of its power.'[11]

Pullman often talks about stories in this way. On another occasion he speaks about story-telling in mystical terms: 'As I write I find myself drifting into a sort of Platonism, as *if the story is there already* like a pure form in some gaseous elsewhere.' Pullman says that he dislikes this Platonism, but that he cannot escape the sense of an obligation, a 'should' that accompanies the task of story-telling.[12] Elsewhere he speaks about 'the controlling intelligence that's telling the story'.[13]

So the writer is a story-*teller* rather than a story-*maker*. The story is not invented or designed by the author. The author's task, rather, is to bring the story into the world, to give it flesh:

> I am the servant of the story – the medium in a spiritualist sense, if you like – and it feels as if, unless I tell this story, I will be troubled and pestered and harried by it and worried and fretted until I do something about it.[14]

This is an interesting belief: the teller is subordinate to the tale. It would be wrong to leap to the conclusion that this reveals an implicit theology, but it certainly begs a series of quasi-theological questions: how does a 'tale' control a 'teller'? Who or what is this cosmic Source who is furnishing Pullman with his stories? What are the rights, freedoms and responsibilities of an author who is acting as 'a medium' on behalf of his story?

According to Pullman, the author's primary responsibility is to the story. Of course the author has other responsibilities as well, but the *unique* responsibility of a story-teller is to 'tell the story'. 'I'm a story-teller, and my responsibility ends here.'[15] This begs so many important questions that Pullman does not answer. If the author's responsibility is simply to 'serve' the story, and if the story comes from elsewhere, then who or what is *responsible* for the story? Who can answer for the story, its attitudes, assumptions, prejudices, portrayals, outcomes and effects? If, for example, a story is offensive, who should answer for that offence? Is it acceptable for the writer to shrug his shoulders and say 'blame it on the story'?

Pullman is insistent on the distance between 'the writer' and 'what is written':

> There is a huge gulf between me, the person, and the book I've written. Of course, I believe in it . . . but the idea that I, Philip Pullman, am somehow accountable for what the characters do or say, or everything that the narrator says, is something I don't believe.[16]

Pullman sees the identification of the author and the narrator as a 'naïve' mistake. 'You mustn't confuse me with the narrator of my novels.'

Pullman is absolutely correct to insist that an author is not responsible for the views and actions of his narrator and characters. After all, it would be absurd to assume that Shakespeare was accountable for Lady Macbeth's views on child-rearing or the political ethics of Cassius. Lady Macbeth is a protagonist not a mouthpiece. However, her character and its progress in the play *is* the product of Shakespeare's artistry. Shakespeare is not accountable for Lady Macbeth's views, but he alone is accountable for her as a literary creation. Shakespeare *is* responsible for creating his characters and the story to which they belong.

The narrator is also a literary creation, although he or she may not feature as a protagonist. In a first person narrative (such as Pullman's *Galatea*) the narrator is visibly and audibly one of the story's characters. The narrator refers to himself, and records his thoughts, feelings and attitudes. In a third person narration, such as *His Dark Materials*, the narrator is much less visible: the narrative voice has no name, never refers to itself, and never draws attention to itself. But the 'third person' narrator is no less a product of the author's making. However hidden or discrete, the narrator's voice must nevertheless be *created*.

Again, Pullman is correct to say that he should not be confused with the narrator of his novels any more than he is to be confused with one of the characters. The narrative voice of *His Dark Materials* is not Pullman's own voice, but a voice created to tell the story. Consequently, the attitudes of his narrator – implicit or otherwise – cannot simply be taken as Pullman's own attitudes.

Having said that, the word 'fiction' derives from the Latin to 'make' or 'fashion'. Whether the stories come from the ether or from the imagination, a writer still *makes* something and is surely accountable in some way for his/her creations. Pullman is responsible for the creation of the narrator. So the way in which the narration proceeds is Pullman's responsibility. He is responsible for the design and creation of his novels, even if he is not to be equated with any individual voice or character. Even if we go along with Pullman's theory that stories are 'given' to him, Pullman is nevertheless responsible for how those stories are told. If the story is told badly or offensively, we can surely hold Pullman accountable – just as, for example, Pullman holds C. S. Lewis accountable for the Narnia series and things 'the narrator' says.

Lies, fantasy and realism

Someone once remarked that the word 'truly' starts with the truth and ends with a lie. Truthfulness in a novel is never simply a question of reporting facts or realities. Telling the truth in a story requires *fiction* – it requires a kind of make-believe or, if you like, 'lying'. One of the themes running through *His Dark Materials* is the exploration of truth-telling and the imagination.

The genesis of this concern with realism and the imagination can be seen much earlier in Pullman's novel *Galatea*, which is a self-conscious experiment with realism. In this novel, Pullman explores the idea that we are connected to reality, even the reality of our human nature, through the imagination: we must *imagine* ourselves and our world in order to make them real. The hero, Martin Browning, is searching for his missing wife but he knows nothing about the circumstances of her disappearance: neither the reason for her departure nor where she has gone. It's this unknown reality that he sets out to uncover. To begin his quest, Browning is forced to follow a hunch. 'A few speculations drifted together' (Gal 1) to give Browning the idea that she must be in Valencia. So Browning's decision is founded in an imaginative guess: as he says, 'I am following omens rather than clues' (Gal 9).

Browning is taken under the wing of a sinister banker called Lionel Pretorius. Pullman introduces Pretorius as 'the broker of reality' because Pretorius' immense wealth has the power to make new realities available. Browning learns that his wife is somehow involved with something called the Anderson Valley Project. With Pretorius' assistance, Browning flies to Venezuela to find the Anderson Valley. His plans are overtaken when a plane crash leaves Browning and his companions stranded in the jungle. From here Browning's quest takes him through a series of unreal societies: a zombie farm and three 'cities of unreal people'.

The First City of unreal people is a technological wasteland peopled by ghosts and Electric Whores. The ghosts are those 'of capitalism . . . of finance, of curiosity' (Gal 122). The whores are the essence of materialism: 'Electricity! Money! Love! Happiness! Matter loving itself' (Gal 125). The Second City is a theocratic state run by a corrupt magistrate. Monks process each day around the banks to 'bless the money' in elaborate cleansing ceremonies. People in the slave class have all been mutilated by a team of surgeons who perform operations of 'manic complexity' (Gal 146), transplanting organs and limbs. Their 'favourite' operation is to produce hermaphrodites.

The first two cities of unreal people only deal in aspects of unreality, but in the Third City *unreality actually is the reality*. Browning finally reaches Anderson Valley or the Perfect City of Unreal People. In this city 'everything is what it seems', but everything is artificial, even the angels (who turn out to be ingenious automata). Sex is banned in the Perfect City and must take place artificially using machines. Browning struggles to find out the 'reality' of the Perfect City, but its reality is its artifice – its lies are the truth. There is no reality, just layer upon layer of falsehood. As the astrologer-magician Vrykolakas says to Browning: 'Pretence everywhere, nothing but lies. If you want to get on in the Perfect City, lie and cheat, that's the thing to do' (Gal 230). Yet Browning manages to find, or make, something real through the love he shares with the angel Galatea who sacrifices her life to save his.

The book ends ironically with Browning becoming a millionaire. Whether this is a good or bad ending,

Pullman does not say. From one point of view, Browning has found material happiness; from another, he has become entangled in the unreality of Lionel Pretorius' capitalist web. We cannot tell whether Browning has found his 'real' self or just another 'unreal self'. The reader is left to contemplate the interdependence of real and imagined worlds.

The use of a series of imaginative cities in *Galatea* is a literary device that goes back at least to John Bunyan's *Pilgrim's Progress*. A more recent example of the genre (and one that may well have influenced Pullman) is Italo Calvino's *Invisible Cities* (1972) in which Marco Polo reports to his master Kublai Khan on numerous unreal cities. The narrator comments at one point: 'The end of every game is a gain or a loss: but of what? What were the real stakes?'[17] This phrase is a very apt summary of the puzzle at the end of *Galatea*. Both Calvino and Pullman raise the issue of realism and then leave it suspended.

Pullman's exploration of dystopic cities of capitalism, technology and sexuality is resonant of J. G. Ballard's *Crash* (1975) where the protagonists have fetishised technology to the extent that they crash their cars for sexual pleasure. In the introduction to *Crash*, Ballard comments on the need for modern novelists to possess a special imaginative power: 'The fiction is already there. The writer's task is to invent the reality.'[18] So the task of the novelist is to 'invent new worlds' that will show us the truth of our everyday world. This is what Pullman strives to do with the Perfect City of Unreal People: he invents a perfectly unreal world in order to reveal the unreality of our late capitalist culture. The imagination offers itself to us as the medium of truth.

In *Galatea* Pullman suggests a general literary theory of the imagination: 'The stronger the imagination, the closer to the reality are the forms it imagines' (Gal 44; cf. 111). This inverts our intuitive belief that the imagination is a flight from reality. We too easily confuse 'imagination' with 'fantasy', argues Pullman. Fantasy is an escape from reality, whereas 'the subtle powerful strength of the imagination is that it deals directly with the real world' (Gal 160).

It is for this reason that Pullman has strongly resisted all descriptions of *His Dark Materials* as 'fantasy literature':

> I don't like fantasy. The only thing about fantasy that interested me when I was writing this was the freedom to invent imagery such as the dæmon; but that was only interesting because I could use it to say something truthful and realistic about human nature. If it was just picturesque or ornamental, I wouldn't be interested.[19]

Pullman insists that he is not like Tolkien whose imaginative world is a self-contained cosmos with an internal logic and coherence. Instead, Pullman has coined the arresting phrase 'stark realism' to describe the genre of *His Dark Materials*.

> By realistic I mean if it is talking about human beings in a way which is vivid and truthful and tells me things about myself and my own emotions and things which I recognise to be true having encountered it in a story. I don't often encounter that sort of thing in fantasy because a lot of fantasy writing seems to me preoccupied with one adventure after another and improbable sorts of magic and weird creatures like orcs and

elves and so on who don't have any connection with the sort of human reality that I recognise, so I am a little bit wary of fantasy and what I was trying to do in my 'fantasy' – and you can probably hear the inverted commas there – was to tell a realistic story by means of the fantastical sort of machinery of the stories.[20]

The difference between fantasy and imaginative realism is crucial for Pullman if he is to give *His Dark Materials* the status of 'myth'. Pullman does not simply want to delight us with his fictional cosmos, he wants us to take the map of his universe and roll it out over the surface of our own world. *His Dark Materials* is an interpretation of our world written in a spirit of 'stark realism'. Pullman is using the term 'realism' in a deliberately provocative way. The 'reality' that Pullman describes in *His Dark Materials* is not the visible world of facts and happenings, but the invisible world of human purposes and desires. The truth of this invisible world can only be told using an imaginative power to create unreal worlds and cities. This is the story-teller's responsibility: not simply to weave tales, but to nourish our imagination with the truth of the human condition.

Lyra is introduced to us in *Northern Lights* as a child with a natural aptitude for deception and story-telling. Lyra's first name sounds like 'liar' – as the harpies in the world of the dead point out – and Iorek Byrnison calls her Silvertongue (NL 348). Yet Lyra is also the agent of truth in the novel, because she alone has the natural ability to read the alethiometer. The word alethiometer is coined from the Greek word for truth (*aletheia*), and it is precisely this word that Jesus uses when he describes himself as 'the way, the truth and the life'. *Aletheia* means 'uncovering' or 'un-forgetting': the truth is something that we find out when fantasy is stripped away. The imagination is the faculty in Lyra that enables her to see through fantasy and falsehood. As the angel Xaphania comments on 'the faculty of imagination': 'that does not mean *making things up*. It is a form of seeing' (AS 523).

The story, the whole story and nothing but the story?

Pullman has become famous not only as a compelling story-teller with a remarkable gift for mythical invention, but – along with Richard Dawkins – as our best known 'cultured despiser' of religion. Pullman does not simply disagree with Christianity, he loathes it, and this fundamental attitude seeps into his fiction. Indeed this attitude is central to the appeal of the *His Dark Materials* trilogy. Pullman confirms to his readers old and young that there is something basically unhealthy and unethical about Christianity and that we would be so much better off without it.

This is, rightly or wrongly, one of the popular tenets of our age: a prejudice against organised religion. Pullman dramatises this prejudice, showing how the good instincts and courage of a young heroine can expose a barbaric church and a pathetic God. Pullman does not offer many new arguments against religion but he provides a myth that embodies a million pub conversations about the pointlessness of God and the hypocrisy of religion. Pullman's readers see their views turned into epic myth.

A *Guardian* feature on Pullman (one of many) said that 'getting the anti-God label has added an edge to Pullman's intellectual credibility, which may account for the huge interest in the Lyra story'.[21] This is, sadly, very true. Criticism of religion is an automatic mark of intellectual interest and credibility. The value of the criticism does not need to be established, because the wrongness of religion is now, for many, a simple and obvious truth that does not need to be questioned.

I arrived at the National Theatre production of *His Dark Materials* dressed in a clerical shirt, having come straight from a meeting at St Paul's Cathedral. I was given grim looks by some other members of the audience who, I can only think, shared Pullman's analysis of Christianity. I was no longer a bloke from Notting Hill out for an evening with my friends: I was an agent of a sinister church organisation intent on suppressing others' freedoms. Or worse.

At a certain point, the criticism of religious oppression can develop an oppressive religious zeal all of its own. Critique itself becomes dogmatic and restrictive. Nowhere has this been more obvious than with Karl Marx. Marx's worthy critique of religion became, in the hands of Marxism, a system of oppression that made the Inquisition look amateurish. Marx thought religion would just wither away naturally as people saw the light of socialism. His successors believed that it must be stamped out.

Pullman has said that his target is really 'religion' in general and that the church is only an example of a general case. 'This is what I'm against. Not Christianity, but every religion and fundamental organisation where there is one truth and they will kill you if you don't believe it.'[22] But it is hard to imagine Pullman casting Judaism or Islam as the villain of *His Dark Materials*. This is because it is recognised that sensitivities in other religions must be respected. Imagine the justified outrage if Pullman had decided to have rabbis or imams

33

kidnapping and killing children! His work would have been rightly labelled racist and xenophobic. And when Pullman lists the numerous names of God in *The Amber Spyglass*, we notice the careful omission of 'Allah' (AS 33).

For some reason launching a category-attack on Christianity is not only culturally accepted, but in many quarters it is applauded. The critique of Christianity does not have to be fair or truthful, let alone sensitive or kind. It's just OK to dislike the church as much as you like, and to feel really righteous about it.

Of course the church has done much to deserve our criticism and distaste. At various times and places the church has been cruel, violent, and dishonest. But the church has also done much that must be admired. It has built schools and hospitals, and set up charitable organisations of every imaginable kind. For centuries the church supported slavery, but it was a Christian who campaigned to abolish it. The church is always struggling unsuccessfully to be its true and best self. And like most historic organisations, the church has a past that mixes glory and shame. The church needs harsh criticism, indeed it should welcome criticism as a stimulus to reform and growth. But the achievements of Christianity also need to be acknowledged, along with the importance of the Christian values of love, forgiveness and social justice.

If we look at secularised cultures we can find many, if not more, examples of barbarism. The two most abhorrent regimes of the last century (arguably the most abhorrent regimes in human history) were the secular empires of Hitler's national socialism and Stalin's communism. These regimes were fuelled by the belief that human beings alone can design and build their own future. Nazism idolised the Aryan hero, who had taken the place of the gods. Stalinist communism idolised the state and its self-preservation.

The fact that non-religious systems can be barbaric too is no comfort to Christianity, which must always be aware of the violence in its own history. But Pullman does not explore the dangers of non-religion in *His Dark Materials*, and lays the blame for human wickedness at the door of religion in general and Christianity in particular.

PART THREE

Themes and Issues

Violence

Looking at all of Pullman's adult or teen fiction, we become aware that he is troubled by the problem of violence. His hero(ine)s often have to resort to violence to achieve noble objectives. This begs the question of a proper non-religious ethic of violence. This is an issue that Pullman explores extensively in much of his fiction, but his exploration does more to illustrate the problem than supply a solution. It is for this reason, perhaps, that Pullman describes literature as a 'school for morals', an experimental space where different ethical scenes can be played out safely.[1]

The Lockhart quartet contains Pullman's first sustained exploration of violence, its misuse and necessities. The problem pivots around the two chief villains: Ah Ling and Axel Bellman. Both of these men are violent and must be overcome by violent means at the hands of the heroine. This splits violence into two categories: the 'bad' violence of the villains and the 'good' violence of the heroine.

Popular fiction normally deals with this dilemma by ensuring that the villains 'earn' any of the violence that must be used against them. The villain must be shown doing something so horrendous, so utterly deserving of retribution or justice, that the hero(ine)'s violence is deemed to be a 'just desert' and not morally problematic. James Bond, for example, is authorised at the end of each movie to destroy his enemies by any violent means available. We do not ask about Bond's ethics, because the villain has, by this stage, been shown to be deserving of annihilation. Bond's 'licence to kill' is not a moral problem, because he is always fighting an absolute and immediate evil. Pullman is too intelligent and sensitive a writer to use such a device. Instead Pullman tries to explore the moral foundations of righteous violence. We see this exploration playing itself out through the Lockhart quartet, *The Butterfly Tattoo* and *His Dark Materials*.

Pullman's hero(ine)s frequently commit, or are implicated in, acts of violence. Martin Browning (in *Galatea*) kills Vrykolakas in the electric lake. Sally Lockhart kills Axel Bellman and shoots Ah Ling. In *His Dark Materials* the alethiometer reveals that Will's defining character is that he is 'a murderer' (SK 29) and his father tells him that his true nature is to be 'a warrior' (AS 440). Will threatens to kill Lyra (SK 64) and shows himself willing to kill the Gallivespian Tialys (AS 177). As the story progresses, Will kills an angel with his knife (AS 30–31) and shoots the leader of the Swiss Guard through the heart (AS 171). Interestingly, Lyra judges Will to be 'a worthy companion' (SK 29) precisely because he is a murderer.

Will wrestles with violence and with his identity as a 'warrior'. The difference between Will's violence and that of Pullman's church is that the church feels good about violence – even providing 'advance absolution' to its assassins. We never see the agents of Pullman's church showing any remorse or even distaste for violence: they plan and execute violence with a righteous pride. By contrast, Will hates violence – Pullman emphasises this repeatedly – and wishes it could stop.

However, Will does not speak for *His Dark Materials*

as a whole. Overall, there is a disturbing ambivalence about violence in the trilogy. Pullman is at pains to let us know that the church's killing of children is morally repugnant, but Lord Asriel's murder of Roger is narrated without any kind of moral comment. We are told, in a brief paragraph, that Lyra is angry about it, and she internally rebukes Lord Asriel with the feeble remark 'how *dare* he?' (NL 397). This is hardly the reaction we would expect from someone who has just seen her best friend killed at the hands of her father. At no point in the trilogy does Pullman pass negative judgement on Asriel. Asriel's crime is never discussed nor is the right-ness of his action ever questioned. Indeed, Lyra takes the blame upon herself, since it was she who unwittingly delivered Roger to Asriel. This is false guilt, of course, although Pullman does not tease this out. (Perhaps there is a Christological reference here, with Lyra paying the price for the sins of her father, but Pullman never makes this explicit.) Nor is the question of Asriel's true guilt for Roger's murder ever raised. At the end of *The Amber Spyglass* (with Roger's murder now long forgotten) Lyra offers the book's obituary to Lord Asriel: 'All that bravery and skill . . . All that, all wasted!' (AS 482). Lyra has absent-mindedly forgotten that Asriel murdered her best friend and forced her to risk her own life to release his soul from the land of the dead.

The moment of Roger's murder is handled by Pullman with narrative sleight of hand. Pullman does not describe Roger's death at Asriel's hands, but instead describes the beautiful, even heavenly, environmental effects that his death produces.

> And high above, the greatest wonder.
> The vault of heaven, star-studded, pro-found, was suddenly pierced as if by a spear.

> A jet of light, a jet of pure energy released
> like an arrow from a great bow, shot upwards.
> The sheets of light and colour that were the
> Aurora tore apart; a great rending, grinding,
> crunching, tearing sound reached from one
> end of the universe to the other; there was
> dry land in the sky –
> Sunlight! (NL 393)

Pullman uses this spectacular environment to symbolise
the nobility and grandeur of Asriel's designs and signals
to the reader that there is a positive value in Roger's murder. Deftly, Pullman shows us the end rather than the
means, inviting us to set Roger's murder against this
magnificent cosmic outcome, thus diverting us from any
problematic moral questions. This is a manipulation of
the reader and a misdirection of our attention. Pullman
holds up in front of us the picture of the Aurora, while
Roger is murdered out of sight.

Roger's death is *necessary* to both to the plot and the
mythic structure of *His Dark Materials*. Pullman's story
requires that a child *must* die in order that Asriel can
generate the energy to break through into another world
and continue his quest to destroy the Authority. Roger's
death is – in Pullman's mythic logic – not so much a *murder* as a *sacrificial killing* carried out in order to achieve a
higher and more noble objective. As Asriel explains just
after taking Roger's life:

> 'This will mean the end of the church . . . the
> end of the Magisterium, the end of all those
> centuries of darkness! Look at that light up
> there: that's the sun of another world! Feel
> the warmth of it on your skin, now!' (NL 394)

Throughout the trilogy Asriel remains an heroic, if

flawed, figure. We are told by John Parry that 'the task [Asriel] has undertaken is the greatest in human history. The greatest in thirty-five thousand years of human history' (SK 224). Pullman encourages us to admire him – it is Asriel after all who brings about the downfall of the Authority. And in the end he dies a hero's death, in hand-to-hand combat with Metatron. But the reader is never invited to analyse Asriel. The other protagonists – even his enemies in the church – either praise him or neglect to pass judgement.

If we compare Pullman's portrayal of Asriel with Milton's portrayal of Satan in *Paradise Lost*, we can see how Milton's treatment is much more nuanced and complex. Milton depicts Satan as utterly depraved, laying out Satan's faults with forensic care. But Milton also offers us a psychology of Satan and his loathing of God: Milton helps us to understand how Satan thinks and feels. This effort to explain the motives for evil and destructiveness powerfully engages our sympathy for Satan. This leaves us with an uncanny tension between Milton's negative moral assessment of Satan and an emotional identification with Satan's personality. Pullman's depiction of Asriel does not leave us with the same complexity of feeling and judgement. Although Pullman shows Asriel as an unfeeling father, he sets all Asriel's faults against the nobility of his grand designs. Pullman guides us away from any moral exploration of Asriel's personality, and encourages us to identify, *without question*, with Asriel's deicidal ambitions.

Roger's death is not the first act of instrumental violence that Pullman does not fully condemn. In the closing pages of *The Shadow in the North*, Sally Lockhart confronts the evil Axel Bellman about the sinking of the *Ingrid Linde* in which many people died. Bellman responds with his theory of utilitarian violence:

> There are poor children . . . who will eat
> and go to school because of what I have
> done. There are families in Mexico who will
> have medical supplies, clean drinking water,
> transport for the produce of their farms,
> security, education . . . I do not regret killing
> those people. If I had not sunk the ship, a
> much greater number would have died – of
> starvation and poverty and ignorance and
> war. It was an act of the highest charity. (SN
> 261–2)

Bellman goes on to offer a justification of his monstrous Steam Machine Gun which protects precisely because of its ultimate horror. Bellman's argument resembles Joseph de Maistre's defence of the executioner. De Maistre argued that violence is everywhere in nature and that the only way to prevent violence in human affairs is to have an ultimate violence, symbolised by a vicious executioner who tortures and mutilates his victims. 'He is no criminal', says de Maistre, because 'all greatness, all power, all social order depends upon the executioner; he is the terror of human society and the tie that holds it together'.[2] Like de Maistre, Bellman sees nature as a play of energy and forces in which violence is simply unavoidable. The only question is how to use the inevitability of violence to bring about peace.

Sally sees in Bellman 'a strange luminous wisdom' (SN 265) and can think of no answer to Bellman's theory, although she believes that somewhere there are arguments 'to refute everything he said' (SN 264). However, Pullman never provides these arguments and the reader is left with Bellman's theory unanswered. *The Butterfly Tattoo* ends in a similar way. Even after Jenny's brutal death, Pullman gives a nod of approval to Carson's argument that 'all the real good in the world' is done by people who are prepared to do evil (BT 156).

It is difficult to square Pullman's moral ambivalence about violence with his scathing condemnation of the train crash in C. S. Lewis' *Chronicles of Narnia*.

> [One of the things] I find particularly objectionable in Lewis [is] the fact that he kills the children at the end. Now here are these children who have gone through great adventures and learned wonderful things and would therefore be in a position to do great things to help other people. But they're taken away. He doesn't let them. For the sake of taking them off to a perpetual school holiday or something, he kills them all in a train crash. I think that's ghastly. It's a horrible message.[3]

If we think back to Roger's death at the bare hands of Lord Asriel, it is difficult to understand Pullman's squeamishness about Lewis' train crash. The train crash is an unpleasant narrative device, and I wouldn't want to defend it – but it is no less unpleasant than Roger having his dæmon torn away. And the train crash victims all go painlessly to heaven, whereas poor Roger ends up in the ghastly land of the dead before disintegrating altogether.

Pullman could have achieved Asriel's objective in any number of ways. He is nothing if not inventive. He could have had Asriel use a special bomb to blast his way through the Aurora, or a newfangled form of transport, or some cutting device like the subtle knife. The possibilities are endless. Of these possibilities Pullman chooses infanticide. The critical reader will very reasonably ask why. It is puzzling that Pullman can see 'the horrible message' in Lewis' *Narnia*, but is oblivious to the unpleasant message in *His Dark Materials*.

Pullman's moral difficulties with violence are connected with his godless universe. With God out of the picture, Pullman's ethics cannot be based upon any theological or metaphysical system of justification. Pullman does not believe in the theological categories of 'good' and 'evil'. So Pullman must explain human conduct in purely human terms: good actions are those which bring about happier human futures. If action A brings about good consequence B, then A is morally justified. So nothing is good in itself, because there is no 'absolute' morality. Good actions are those that produce, or appear to produce, or can be *interpreted* as producing, 'good' consequences.

Consequentialist ethics are further complicated by the difficulty of defining both what is 'good' and what is a 'consequence'. Human history shows us that the term 'good' can be made to apply (by someone-or-other) to everything from the welfare state to the invasion of Iraq. What counts as the true 'good' is by no means universally agreed. And *everything* is a 'consequence' in the great chain-reaction of human causes and effects. A complex range of effects flows from every human action. So we can say that the creation of the Eastern Bloc was one consequence of the Second World War, but so was the creation of the European Union. At what point in the multiple unfolding sequences of effects do we decide that *the* consequences of our action have become clear?

Consequentialist ethics are also a difficult game for anyone who does not have the gift of seeing the future. Unfortunately, the inability to see the future is part of the human condition. We are not clairvoyant and must proceed by *guessing* at the future consequences of our actions. These guesses are frequently wrong. Instinctively, Pullman knows that the problem of the future is at the centre of his godless ethical universe.

So he gives Lyra a device, the alethiometer, which can help her to work out what will happen. This means that Lyra – and in turn Pullman's young readers – never have to face the unnerving realities of doing ethics without God.

Pullman thinks it would be better for us to live in a world where only human projects matter. But if the point of our lives is to bring about good outcomes, then good outcomes will become the criteria for good moral conduct. The 'good person' is the one who achieves good things. This consequentialist ethic is every bit as morally problematic as a religious ethic of virtue or duty – the risk is that human lives can become mere instruments of a higher purpose, like poor Roger. Roger's death is morally evaluated against Asriel's success. Because Asriel succeeds, Roger's murder is OK. Consequentialist ethics turns morality into an endless calculation: adding up the benefits of an action and subtracting the drawbacks. If the benefits score higher, the action becomes 'good'; if the drawbacks score higher the action is 'bad'. Pullman never fully endorses this ethic, but neither does he criticise it – whether with Bellman or Carson or Asriel.

Pullman's ambivalence about the ethics of violence reveals a deeper theological ambivalence. On the one hand Pullman objects to a divine authority who lays down the moral law. On the other hand he is not entirely comfortable with an ethic worked out in purely human terms. So he is left giving two cheers to ethics without God. It nearly works; but not quite. Not unless you have an alethiometer – but in real life, alethiometers are in rather short supply. The 'stark reality' for us is rather more complicated.

Pullman's church

Although Pullman denies the charge of being a sermon-ising atheist, *His Dark Materials* vibrates with a preacher's zeal and purpose. Pullman depicts the church as a child-murdering conspiracy and God as a feeble idiot. Pullman urges us to follow the example of his heroine and work towards a 'republic of heaven' built with human hands and free from the oppression of religious ideology. Pullman would concur with the observation of Karl Marx that the criticism of religion is the basis of all criticism: religion is the primary obstacle to human growth, blocking both personal development and cultural progress.

We learn early on in *Northern Lights* that the church is conducting experiments that resemble some of the medical atrocities of the Nazis. Children have been confined in an Arctic camp where they are tested for Dust and subjected to an operation called 'intercision' that separates them from their dæmons and results in a slow, tormented death. This is an atrocity equivalent, Pullman tells us, to removing someone's face or tearing his heart out (NL 215). Pullman uses 'intercision' as a symbol for an ultimate atrocity, an ultimate de-humani-sation. As Lyra's friend, the witch Serafina Pekkala, puts it, 'cutting children's dæmons away [is] the most evil work I've ever heard of' (SK 43). The hideously evil Mrs Coulter is in charge of the child camp and its experi-ments. But she does this with the full authority of the church. 'Where there are priests, there is fear of Dust', explains Serafina Pekkala (NL 318). This fear translates itself into violence and cruelty.

The character of 'intercison' echoes Pullman's basic charge against Christianity: Christianity tries to separate us from the experiences that make us human. The church calls these experiences 'sinful' and tries to cut us off from them. Intercison is not just an excess perpetrated by someone at the fringe of the establishment. The atrocity is an extension of church policy, a reflection of the doctrine of original sin.

The church of *His Dark Materials* is an amalgam of Catholic and Protestant Christianity; the structures all have a Catholic flavour (the Magisterium, the Inquisition, the Oblation Board etc.) but are located in Geneva, the birthplace of Calvinism. In this way Pullman makes it clear that his attack is not on this or that church, but on 'church' in general. The church is also shown in alliance with all the apparatus of a police state: secret organisations, agents, soldiers, sinister technologies. Pullman tells us that 'every philosophical research establishment . . . had to include on its staff a representative of the Magisterium, to act as a censor and suppress the news of any heretical discoveries' (SK 130). This is the only view of the church that Pullman provides in *His Dark Materials*. The church is evil through and through. There are no good priests, no good actions, indeed no mitigating evidence whatsoever. Pullman shows the church as a solidly wicked entity. In an interview for Christian Aid, Pullman explains that the cruelty of religion is 'a universal law'.

> But when you look at organised religion of whatever sort – whether it's Christianity in all its variants, or whether it's Islam or some forms of extreme Hinduism – wherever you see organised religion and priesthoods and power, you see cruelty and tyranny and repression. It's almost a universal law.[4]

Pullman repeatedly shows his characters experiencing nausea after encountering the church: a 'spasm of disgust' crosses the face of Lord Asriel when he hears 'talk of the sacraments, and atonement, and redemption, and suchlike' (SK 47). Will 'feels sick' after his encounter with the priest Semyon (AS 106). Lee Scoresby considers the Skraeling's 'martyrdom' with 'distaste' (SK 132). The effect at every turn is to reinforce an attitude of complete revulsion.

There is a curious episode in *The Amber Spyglass* when Will is trying to make his way back to Lyra. On his journey Will passes through a 'shabby' village with a 'church' in it. In the village he is invited to drink vodka by the local priest. Will declines the priest's offer of accommodation for the night, and presses on filled with a nausea that lasts for hours. This episode is redundant to the overall drama of the story. Will learns nothing that he can use later on, nor does this encounter have a special significance in the light of future events. So why does Pullman put this passage in?

The key function of this episode is not to tell the story but to offer the reader a portrait of the local clergy. We have seen the church hierarchy at work in Geneva and we have seen devious agents of the church, like Mrs Coulter, doing their foul work. But Pullman's horror showcase of church cruelty would not be complete without showing the evil character of the village parson. And the village parson Pullman shows us is truly repulsive. He has 'fat dirty fingers', 'food-stains on his cassock' (AS 106) and emits 'vapours of tobacco and alcohol and sweat'. After lunch, the priest treats Will to an *ad hoc* sermon about witches:

> 'Witches – daughters of evil! The church should have put them all to death many years ago. Witches – have nothing to do with them . . . you hear me . . . They will try to

> seduce you . . . They will take your future,
> your children that are to come and leave you
> nothing. They should be put to death, every
> one.' (AS 105)

The sexual undertow continues as Will is invited to share a bottle of vodka. The priest – who has 'restless eyes' that 'moved over Will's face and body, taking everything in' – is overtly physical, putting an arm around Will's shoulder and stroking Will's arm and knee (AS 102–3). Will leaves the priest's house with his 'head swimming' and 'stomach lurching' (AS 107). The priest is a grotesque figure and the reader is left feeling nearly as sick as Will.

The point of this vignette is to show that the depravity of the church goes all the way down from the Magisterium to the parish clergy. In case the reader is in any doubt by the third volume of the trilogy, Pullman gives additional confirmation that there really are no good people anywhere in the church. As Serafina Pekkala tells us, 'Every church is the same: control, destroy, obliterate every good feeling' (SK 52).

In this episode the story takes a back seat to the sermon. If this episode were removed there would be no loss whatsoever to the progress of the narrative: Will would still get his job done and the drama would still hang together. This episode serves principally as Pullman's way-side pulpit: a platform for the ideological intentions of the author.

On a larger scale, the entire Mary Malone plot serves a similar (if not so obvious) ideological purpose. Mary Malone is a university researcher into dark matter who is introduced in *The Subtle Knife*. As a result of meeting Lyra, Mary becomes entangled in the wider conflict and her life is threatened. She is forced to leave her job and, guided by messages from angels, is taken to safety into a parallel world. And she remains in this parallel world until the main action of the novel is finished.

Mary's journey to the world of the Mulefa is a skilful imaginative set piece. Pullman shows, again, his quirky inventiveness by sketching a world peopled by wheeled elephants whose existence is threatened because Dust is drifting in the wrong direction and interfering with their delicate ecosystem. Mary, as a result of her research into Dust/dark matter, is able to help them with the aid of an instrument she makes herself: the 'amber spyglass', which enables her to see Dust. This is all very interesting. But this story is not so much a sub-plot as a parallel plot, which contributes nothing to the main narrative. The rescue of the Mulefa makes no difference to the outcome of the story. Interesting as Mary's character is, she is largely redundant to the structure of the main plot.

In the National Theatre stage-adaptation of *His Dark Materials*, both the Mary Malone sub-plot and the paedophile priest episode were dropped entirely and this made no difference to the main lines and themes of the story. Unlike Serafina Pekkala, whose goose-dæmon frequently turns up to get Lyra out of a tight corner, Mary Malone spends most of her time in a parallel universe and plays no part in the fulfilment of Lyra's destiny. When Mary reappears in the main narrative, towards the end of *The Amber Spyglass*, Lyra and Will have already released the spirits of the dead, seen Metatron destroyed, and watched God wither and die. There is nothing left for Mary to do: the mission has been accomplished.

The Mary Malone plot does give Pullman an opportunity to elaborate on the theory of Dust and its connections with quantum physics. But more importantly, Mary provides Pullman with the opportunity to include speeches and conversations about the errors of

Christianity. Mary is an ex-nun and, in the chapter 'Marzipan', she explains how the discovery of her sexuality led her to abandon Christianity. Pullman does this well, making some telling points, but the reader is left asking what role this conversation plays in the novel.

Lyra, who has seen the church at its most barbaric, hardly needs any additional evidence that Christianity is very bad for you. Pullman has made this abundantly clear already. But Pullman is like a dog with a bone: he wants to tell us – in still more detail, from another angle, and out of the mouth of yet another protagonist – just how very negative and pointless Christianity is.

And Pullman is very good, very persuasive, at presenting his arguments against Christianity. He has carefully developed Mary Malone as a sympathetic character. She is an intelligent woman who has saved an endangered species. The joyful, peace-loving, monogamous Mulefa are 'full of gratitude' (AS 139) to Mary. By the time we read her criticisms of the church, she has earned the reader's profound respect. Who could contradict such a paragon? Again we see Pullman putting the needs of ideology before the needs of the story. The story does not need Mary Malone's sexual history, but Pullman needs to tell us. Pullman wants to add a further dimension to his scathing critique of Christianity.

Looking back to *Galatea*, we can see an earlier attempt to create an alternative world controlled by the church. In *Galatea*, Pullman imagines an unpleasant politico-religious system ('The Second City of Unreal People') which is governed by 'His Catholic Excellency Don Alvaro', a pompous midget who is guided by the officials of the church. The city is policed by monks with rifles and serviced by a farm, which is hidden in a network of mountain tunnels. The farm is worked by blasphemers who are being punished for crimes against the church. These 'convicts' have the 'fearsome task' of cleaning the excrement from the animal pens:

> But nature had provided a waste-disposal system of sorts; a cavern had been discovered in the very depths of the mountain, in the centre of which was a fissure that had no measurable bottom. It had been calculated by the Bishop's committee that shit could be deposited in there with perfect safety until the year 2000, when the Lord Jesus Christ himself would return with further instructions. (Gal 161)

The allegorical meaning is pretty obvious: the mountain is a hell of the church's making. Instead of liberating people to live freely and creatively, religion traps people into thinking that they must dedicate their lives to cleaning out the excremental stain of original sin.

Some commentators have said that since there is no Jesus in *His Dark Materials*, Pullman is not really criticising Christianity, but pernicious aspects of the church. We could also say that Pullman's church is a fiction in another world and therefore not really a critique of the real church. We might add that Pullman's depictions of the church are just story-telling. After all, Lyra needs to fight a truly worthy cause – and what could be more worthy than preventing child-murder? The 'church' just happens to be the organisation murdering children, but the story could have been told in other ways.

To an extent all this is true. But it would be a mistake to think that in writing about an imaginary church, Pullman is not trying to criticise the real church or real Christianity. Jesus does not feature in *His Dark Materials*, but there are many references to real Christianity: Father

Gomez, the cool, determined priest-assassin sent to kill Lyra, carries with him an explicitly Christian symbol: 'The crucifix around his neck and the rifle at his back were twin tokens of his absolute determination to complete the task' (AS 290).

Mary Malone expresses her rejection of religion by taking the crucifix from around her neck and throwing it into the sea (AS 469). Without Mary Malone, we could just about plausibly argue that Pullman's church is an other-worldly fantasy. But Mary comes from our world. The Christianity she criticises is the church of our world. Indeed, as I have argued, this is her principal function: to fill out Pullman's critique of religion by sketching in the link between Lyra's fantastic church and the churches of our world. Let us also remember Pullman's 'stark realism'. Pullman does not write fantasy, but imaginative stories that seek to tell us something true about the real world.

We need to look, though, at what lies behind Pullman's over-the-top portrayal of Christianity. It is not simply that Pullman wants to reject Christianity as a 'convincing mistake' (AS 464), he wants to *replace* Christianity with a more perfect world-view: he wants to supplant the Christian myth with his own story of human salvation. Alongside the critique of the church, Pullman is constantly dropping hints about an alternative, post-Christian 'religious' attitude. We will not be saved by God or the church, but by realising our human potential for good and building the republic of heaven. There is no God, but there is something called Dust or the self-consciousness of the cosmos. Mary Malone's 'spiritual life' is empty, but Lyra and her dæmon enjoy a rich 'spiritual' relationship. There is no divine plan, but nevertheless there are human 'destinies' that must be taken seriously.

The soul

> Man's character is his dæmon.
> (Heraclitus)[5]

In Lyra's world, everyone has his or her soul on the outside, in the form of an animal dæmon. This dæmon is attached to the person by a powerful bond. The dæmons can talk, and move independently so long as they remain in proximity to their human partner. Pullman says that he took the idea of a dæmon from Socrates who liked to talk about what he called his *'daimonion'*.

Socrates wrote nothing himself and we encounter him principally through Plato's descriptions and portrayals. Plato sees the *daimonion* as a 'companion' who 'lends support' or 'co-operates' in educating the human partner in his or her engagement with the *Logos*. The *daimonion* is a guiding star that 'speaks' to the human soul, leading it towards the truth. Plato also says that Socrates saw his *daimonion* as 'a divine element' and 'the sign of a god'.[6] In the *Symposium*, Love is described as a dæmonic spirit 'halfway between god and humanity' that mediates between heaven and earth. 'It is only through the mediation of the spirit world that humans can have any intercourse . . . with the gods.'[7]

Interestingly, Pullman sees no religious significance in his notion of a dæmon. However, Pullman does play with the religious resonances of the word dæmon, particularly the aural similarity with the 'demons' that religion sees as 'evil'. Pullman asserts a very positive and life-affirming idea of the dæmonic in place of the church's negative idea of demonic possession. The process of 'intercision', in *Northern Lights*, where children are forcibly separated from their dæmons, is a form of exorcism designed to rid the children of the 'evil' of Dust.

Pullman's invention of dæmons is surely the crowning achievement of *His Dark Materials*. Dæmons enable Pullman to narrate in the most vivid way the developing inner life of his protagonists. Pullman uses the dæmons to dramatise soliloquy and the growth of external relationships. The dæmons also supply an explanation of the difference between adults and children.

> I was still discovering new things I could do with this idea right up until the last pages of this book. It was a very sort of rich idea with all kinds of implications and meanings in it. One of the things people are struck most by is the fact that children's dæmons can change shapes, whereas adult dæmons have settled into one shape and keep it the rest of their lives. I found that a very good way of demonstrating the difference between children and grown-ups, between innocence and experience – the sort of infinite potentiality children have, the great malleability of their characters. They change very quickly, their moods change. Grown-ups don't have that. We've lost that.[8]

A number of commentators have described Pullman's dæmons as 'transitional objects'.[9] The term 'transitional object' was coined by the psychologist D. W. Winnicott to describe the cuddly toys, blankets and other 'comforters' to which young children become very attached. Winnicott argued that children use these objects to negotiate their separation from the mother. The transitional object is a safe, controlled 'other' that gives the child security and confidence when the mother is not present. The transitional object also enables a child to soliloquise by 'talking to teddy' and thereby to engage in self-reflection. Pullman frequently uses Lyra's dæmon in such a way to dramatise soliloquy and internal dissonance.

The transitional object allows the child to begin experimenting in the 'transitional space' between itself and the wider world. Because the dæmons can change, this gives a powerful sense of children trying out new personae, new feelings and new world-views. Lyra's changing dæmon is the way in which she can test out versions of herself in the external world. In adulthood, these rehearsals and experiments are stabilised in the person's fixed dæmon.

Rowan Williams has recently warned that this 'transitional space' of childhood experimentation is now being threatened by cultural pressure to treat children as adults. 'Children need to be free of the pressure to make adult choices if they are ever to *learn* how to make adult choices.'[10] Children must be allowed to play at making choices in a realm which is free of the real economic, sexual and political pressures that condition adult life. The entire universe of *His Dark Materials* could be seen as an imaginative 'transitional space' in which the child-hood reader can follow Lyra's story as a safe experiment in adulthood. Lyra is given an adult task, and she is exposed to adult scenarios: cruelty, violence, danger and the awareness of her own sexuality. But she has the com-fort of her dæmon (her transitional object) and she is protected not only by powerful adults, but by magical instruments and angelic agents. Lyra's experiment in adulthood is thoroughly managed and controlled by Pullman using a range of literary devices.

Winnicott describes 'transitional space' as 'the space between inner and outer worlds, which is also the space between people [in which] intimate relationships and creativity occur'.[11] Pullman uses Will and Lyra's dæmons as a way of narrating their developing intimacy and growth into adulthood. In normal human development, children let go of their 'comforters' in order to form grown-up relationships with others. Similarly, when Lyra and Will enter the land of the dead they must lose their dæmons. And it is while they are both bereft of their 'transitional objects' that their intimate relationship begins to develop: Mary Malone tells the children of her sexual development and this provokes Will and Lyra to explore the meaning and purpose of their bodies. Pullman sets the scene with a sumptuous meal prepared by the Mulefa (AS 451). Lyra and Will bathe naked in the river (AS 458–9), and 'the whole landscape [is] aquiver with life' (AS 462). As Mary speaks about her first sexual encounter,

> Lyra felt something strange happen to her body. She felt a stirring at the roots of her hair: she found herself breathing faster . . . the sensations in her breast . . . were exciting and frightening at the same time and she had not the slightest idea why. (AS 467)

Later, still separated from their dæmons, Will and Lyra make love (AS 492). The emotional and psychological progress to this point is managed perfectly by Pullman.

When the dæmons return, they have been altered by their experience. The dæmons have been talking with an angel called Xaphania who persuades them to act as the children's voice of conscience and responsibility. The dæmons are no longer 'comforters' in the childish sense but alter egos urging Will and Lyra to meet their wider responsibilities to humanity. Pullman is less effective in explaining how the dæmons make this change.

Winnicott argues that this stage in the exploration of transitional space is not only ethical but religious. As children (and indeed adults) progress, they develop a 'religious' sense of the abstract 'otherness' that constitutes objective experience. The transitional space not only includes the potential for intimacy with other persons, but intimacy with the Other in general.

At various points in the trilogy, Pullman tries to express this sense of cosmic 'otherness'. When Asriel breaks through the Aurora, Lyra stands in wonder at the 'sun of [another] world . . . shining into this' (NL 397). Again, when the children emerge from the land of the dead and the ghosts of the dead dissolve into the cosmos, Lyra and Will experience 'every nerve in their bodies blessing the sweetness of the good soil, the night air, the stars' (AS 382). But most significantly, Mary Malone has an out-of-body experience when she is caught in a powerful current of Dust (AS 384–7). As a result she realises that

> she herself was partly Shadow-matter. Part of her was subject to this tide that was moving through the cosmos. And . . . so were human beings in every world, and every kind of conscious creature, wherever they were. (AS 386–7)

This experience, in Winnicott's terms, is the ultimate encounter in transitional space, where one's own self is experienced as just one small part of everything else. Mary makes the complete transition from 'self' into 'other'. This accords very much with Plato's understanding of the *daimonion* as that which guides us towards a universal world-view.

Don Cupitt has argued that this cosmic feeling is the new, non-real, religious experience.[12] At certain moments we have a sense of 'The Meaning of It All': we are part of 'It All' and 'It All' is part of us. This experience is religious, but it does not require the existence of God. Life, the cosmos, everything – this is the new religious object. Perhaps this is what Pullman has in mind, although I suspect that Pullman would see no reason to call this experience religious.

Pullman may not see any religious significance in this 'cosmic feeling', but there are many resonances with mystical religious experience. Meister Eckhart, for example, wrote

> As long as I am this or that, or have this or that, I am not all things and I have not all things. Become pure till you neither have this or that; then you are omnipresent and, being neither this nor that, are all things.[13]

Pullman's concern with 'It All' begs the question that will be explored at the end of this book: to what extent does Pullman's trilogy reveal an implicit theology? Pullman's dæmons are not just a charming narrative device, but raise important philosophical and religious issues about human development, human identity and the place of human beings in the ultimate cosmic picture.

Dust

> Vast is the kingdom of dust!
> Unlike terrestrial kingdoms, it knows no
>   limits.
>   (J. Gordon Ogden, *The Kingdom of Dust*)[14]

Part of Pullman's literary genius is his ability to capture nebulous and complex ideas in a clear and compelling image. The dæmon, for example, embodies the realm of inner experience: the soul, the self, wishes and desires, hopes and fears, ambivalence and tension. Pullman also has a concept to embrace the idea of the 'world soul', or the essence of human experience: Dust.

The word 'dust' carries a complex range of contradictory connotations and resonances. We are immediately reminded of the 'dust' from which Adam is formed in Genesis: 'Then the Lord God formed man from the dust of the ground, and breathed into his nostrils the breath of life; and the man became a living soul' (Genesis 2:7, AV). Dust is primitive matter, pre-human and prelapsarian. It originates in pre-history and comes together into a human form to create history: 'dust thou art, and unto dust shalt thou return' (Genesis 3:19, AV).

For the English poets of the early seventeenth century, 'dust' was simply 'death': 'Golden lads and girls all must, / As chimney-sweepers, come to dust.'[15] Yet dust also conjures up a sense of magic and innocence. Joni Mitchell saw dust as the essence of natural human goodness: 'We are stardust / We are golden / And we've got to get ourselves / Back to the garden.'[16]

To think of ourselves as 'dust' places us in a cosmic perspective. We are in the end – and in the beginning – just particles of matter. For a few fleeting years we come together into a human shape before disintegrating back into the swirl of particles that makes up the cosmos. So the word 'dust' has become a metaphor for the frailty and transience of the human body. But not just the human body: all things become dust. Even diamonds wear down. And where does all that diamond dust go? Everything wears down. Dust is an emblem of the inevitable corruptibility of matter.

Dust is also 'dirt' and Pullman's church sees Dust as the dirt of original sin: the corrupt basis of human nature that must be cut out and destroyed. In our every-day lives, dust is what we wipe away in order to have a clean, fresh environment. Dust keeps settling, and we keep brushing it away, in an everlasting contest. And we know in the end that dust will win: 'Vast is the kingdom of dust!'

Pullman takes this wonderfully suggestive substance and connects it with scientific theories about the composition of the universe. The association of Dust with 'dark matter' in *His Dark Materials* is a flight of fancy, but it does have a kind of scientific plausibility. Since the ancient Greek atomists Leucippus and Democritus, scientists have been fascinated by the question of fundamental particles. With the invention of the microscope in 1590, the investigation of previously invisible components of matter slowly started to become possible. The microcosmic world of 'dust' started to come into focus, and smaller and smaller particles were discovered. A deeper understanding of the 'dust' that makes up matter is one of the major achievements of modern science.

Dust is also linked conceptually with the idea of other worlds. With the development of the microscope the idea of microcosms, or miniature versions of our own world, became fashionable. The philosopher Blaise Pascal was, for one, a strong believer in the reality of microcosms: 'infinities of universes' within each particle of dust in our world. Pullman has not cited microcosmic theory as a source, but perhaps he was influenced by William Blake who urged us 'to see a world in a grain of sand'.

There is a more particular and surprising source for Pullman's idea of Dust: C. S. Lewis' *Chronicles of Narnia*. Pullman has not mentioned Lewis' reference to dust, but it is hard to imagine that he is not aware that Uncle Andrew, in *The Magician's Nephew*, talks about a mysterious substance called 'dust' that comes from another world:

> Although there was not really the least chance of anyone overhearing them, he leaned forward and almost whispered as he said:
>
> 'The Atlantean box contained something that had been brought from another world when our world was only just beginning.'
>
> 'What?' asked Digory, who was now interested despite of himself.
>
> 'Only dust,' said Uncle Andrew. 'Fine, dry dust. Nothing much to look at. Not much to show for a lifetime of toil, you might say. Ah, but when I looked at that dust (I took jolly good care not to touch it) and thought that every grain had once been in another world – I don't mean another planet, you know; they're part of our world and you could get to them if you went far enough – but a really Other World – another Nature – another universe – somewhere you would never reach even if you travelled through the space of this universe for ever – a world that could be reached only by Magic – Well!' Here Uncle Andrew rubbed his hands till his knuckles cracked like fireworks.[17]

Uncle Andrew fashions the dust into yellow and green rings that enable transport between different worlds. In *His Dark Materials* we read that Lord Asriel is using Dust 'in order to make a bridge between this world and the world beyond the Aurora' (NL 188).

Pullman uses this complex network of resonances and associations to give density and texture to his notion of

'Dust'. At the beginning of *Northern Lights*, Lyra realises that Dust is a crucial substance at the centre of the scientific and religious politics of her world. Her father, Lord Asriel, is conducting controversial experiments with Dust and Lyra is immediately fascinated. The reader is drawn into Lyra's curiosity and Pullman slowly discloses the truth about Dust as the trilogy develops. The full significance of Dust for the future of human history is only revealed in the very last chapters of *The Amber Spyglass*.

In Genesis dust is just raw, inert matter that God fashions into life. Dust is all that there would be if God had not breathed life into the cosmos. Pullman turns all this on its head. Dust is not the raw material of life, but processed life, life that has gone through the wringer of human trial and error. God has nothing to do with Dust, because Dust is *what we make* by living the human life. Dust is what conscious life gives off by developing, erring, creating and learning. Dust is the very essence of what it means to be human. Dust is described as enlightenment (AS 235), 'spirit' (SK 260), 'particles of consciousness' (SK 92) and 'matter understanding itself' (AS 33).

Pullman's church fears Dust, because it fears real human experience. Lord Asriel tells Lyra that 'Dust was the physical evidence for original sin' (NL 371). Dust is a sign of experience, knowledge and human development. But the church idolises innocence because it associates experience with error, and error with sin. In separating children from their dæmons, the church believes that it is 'saving' them from sin. However, what the church calls 'sin' is in fact just the normal human experience of growing up. The church's fear of Dust is really just a fear of 'being human'.

Dust is the central metaphysical concept in *His Dark*

Materials. Hegel tried to express something similar with his concept of *Geist* (meaning 'mind' or 'spirit'). *Geist* is the evolution of human freedom. Because *Geist* is free it develops through free human choices. *Geist* synthesises human error into something positive, using experience to create the conditions for a better human future. *Geist* can do this because it is *rational*. What Hegel called 'the cunning of reason' turns all our worst faults and mistakes to positive advantage. *Geist* follows a haphazard course, but despite mishaps it just keeps on winning, taking humanity forwards.

Hegel's *Geist* is not only the energy of experience but the essence, too, of human history. *Geist* has an internal logic that progressively pushes human affairs towards a 'good infinity'. Pullman's Dust works in an analogous way, animating the alethiometer which can see forward in time and thereby direct Lyra to fulfil her destiny and the true human future: the republic of heaven (NL 183).

The significant difference between Pullman and Hegel is that Hegel explicitly connects *Geist* with God. *Geist* is the Holy Spirit working itself out through human history. God is 'the eternal process' of the created order.[18] By contrast, Pullman sees Dust as the opposite of divinity. Yet we cannot help wondering whether Dust isn't disguising an underlying 'theology' in Pullman.

Sexuality

> Virtual or immediate touch?
> (Milton, *Paradise Lost*)[19]

Looking at Pullman's adult and teenage writing as a whole, we can see that sexuality is one of his central preoccupations. Pullman is intrigued by intimacy in what Milton called its 'immediate' (physical) and 'virtual' (spiritual) forms. In *The Haunted Storm*, Pullman explores the tension between intimacy and distance in the relationship between Matthew and Elizabeth. Matthew has sex with Elizabeth within a few minutes of meeting her, but their relationship thereafter is chaste and 'spiritual'. The two lovers seem to find a greater closeness in their non-physical relationship than in the empty sexual act of their first meeting. In *Galatea*, the hero Martin Browning has a relationship with an 'angel' who possesses an ambiguous, unreal body. Their sexual encounter takes place in an ambiguous space half-way between the body and the imagination. In both these early novels, Pullman tries to explore sexuality beyond mere physicality, looking at the function of the imagination in sexuality and the intimacy created by language, images and the distance between bodies.

These themes re-surface in *His Dark Materials*, where Pullman (carefully mindful of his childhood audience) explores the sexual intimacy between Lyra and Will, and between the angels Baruch and Balthamos. Lyra and Will 'make love' twice: on the first occasion their bodies touch (but without their dæmons) after Lyra has fed Will one of the mysterious 'sweet, thirst-quenching red fruits' that Mary Malone has given her (AS 481 and 492); on the second occasion they reach out to touch each other's dæmons. It is this second, more 'spiritual' intimacy that feels the most powerful and intense:

> Will put his hand on hers . . . knowing exactly
> what he was doing and exactly what it
> would mean, he moved his hand from Lyra's
> wrist and stroked the red-gold fur of her
> dæmon.
>
> Lyra gasped. But her surprise was mixed
> with a pleasure so like the joy that had

flooded through her when she had put the
fruit to his lips that she couldn't protest,
because she was breathless. With a racing
heart she responded in the same way: she put
her hand on the silky warmth of Will's
dæmon. (AS 527–8)

Here the touching of the dæmons clearly represents
erogenous contact. But this exchange of touches is also a
metaphor for an intimacy that includes the physical but
transcends bodily contact. Here Lyra and Will make contact, symbolically, with each other's private, inner and
vulnerable selves.

Pullman takes up this theme elsewhere in the trilogy
through the relationship between the angels Baruch and
Balthamos. Will sees the angels holding each other,
hovering near the campfire:

The two angels were embracing, and Will,
gazing into the flames, saw their mutual affection. More than affection: they loved each
other with a passion. (AS 27)

The possibility of sex with angels has already been raised
in *Galatea* where the angel's indefinite, quasi-physical
body fascinates Pullman. Here again Pullman explores
the idea of a sexual love which extends beyond our ordinary ideas of bodily contact. Pullman leaves the angels'
physical status deliberately ambiguous: they possess
'shapes' but do not have 'true flesh' (AS 11–12). They are
transparent and can move like gas. Moreover, the bond
between the angels transcends space, so that when one
angel is killed, the other immediately feels the pain.
Pullman presents their love, and their sexuality, as the
purest kind of interpersonal relationship.

Pullman may well have taken his inspiration from

Milton, who raises the question of angelic sexuality in *Paradise Lost*. In the long section in which the angel Raphael is responding to Adam's questions, Adam asks whether angels can enjoy sexual relationships.

> 'Bear with me, then, if lawful what I ask.
> Love not the heavenly spirits? and how their
>   love
> Express they? by looks only? or do they mix
> Irradiance, virtual or immediate touch?'
> To whom the angel, with a smile that glow'd
> Celestial rosy red, love's proper hue,
> Answered: 'Let it suffice thee that thou
>   know'st
> Us happy, and without love no happiness.
> Whatever pure thou in body enjoy'st
> (And pure thou wert created) we enjoy
> In eminence, and obstacle find none
> Of membrane, joint or limb, exclusive bars;
> Easier than air with air, if spirits embrace,
> Total they mix, union of pure with pure
> Desiring.'[20]

Given Milton's puritan theology, this passage is a wonderfully unexpected affirmation of sexuality, implying that sexual pleasure is even better in heaven than it is on earth.

We can see why this passage would appeal to Pullman, because Milton suggests that true sexuality involves the 'virtual' body more than the 'immediate' body of flesh. Pullman never says that he is exploring the 'spirituality' of sexuality, but this surely is what he is doing. Pullman's angels represent the spirituality of sex, the essence of what Milton calls 'love's proper hue', a 'union of pure with pure desiring'.

It would certainly be unfair to see the 'spirituality'

of sexuality as a theological theme. But there is a theological flavour to Pullman's concern with the essence and spirit of sexual relationships. Pullman may dismiss God, but he still wants the world to be a spiritually enchanted place. The material world is not enough for him: it has to be showered with Dust. The material body is not enough: it has to have a dæmon. And the sexual interaction of bodies is not enough: it must have a spiritual meaning.

Innocence and experience

> Folly is an endless maze,
> Tangled roots perplex her ways,
> How many have fallen there!'
> (William Blake, 'The Voice of an Ancient Bard')

In his teen novel, *The Butterfly Tattoo*, Pullman writes a tremendous set-piece temptation scene that echoes and revises the temptation episode in Genesis. The young hero Chris Marshall is caught up in a complex plot involving terrorism and the criminal underworld. In a conversation with the villain (Carson) Chris is persuaded, in the cause of national security, to betray his friend Barry. Carson offers Chris this justification for the betrayal:

> 'I don't know if you're religious. The Garden of Eden – you know that story? The tree of knowledge of good and evil. Remember that? Before you eat the fruit you're innocent, whatever you do is innocent, because you don't understand. Then you eat it. You *know* now. And you are never innocent again. And that's painful; it's a terrible thing. I know

what I'm asking you, Chris. I am asking you
to betray a man you thought was a friend. I
am asking you to taste the fruit.

'But I'll tell you something. Losing that
innocence is the first step on the road to real
knowledge. To wisdom, if you like, You can't
get wisdom till you lose that innocence . . .
Those people out there – innocent, because
they don't know. Like children. Like sheep.
No sheep can do evil, because it's innocent,
right? But no sheep can do good, either. If
you don't know what it is you can't do it. So
it's paradoxical, isn't it? You can't do good
unless you stop being innocent. All the real
good in the world is done by the people
who've tasted the fruit of that tree. And
found it bitter and painful.' (BT 155–6)

Carson's logic turns out to be ironic, because for all
this talk of experience, Chris is still an innocent dupe.
The person who is telling him about the necessity of
betrayal is at that very moment betraying him. Chris
thinks he is acting on experience: in fact he is acting out
of his naïvety. This naïvety leads to the tragic death of
Chris's girlfriend Jenny. Later, after Jenny has been shot
by Carson, Chris reflects upon his earlier conversation.

In his solitude, he often thought about what
Carson had said to him as they sat in the
white Mercedes, about innocence, about good
and evil. It was very strange. Carson had
appealed to the highest part of him, not the
lowest, and although the wisdom he spoke
came from the tongue of a liar, still it was the
truest wisdom Chris had ever heard. (BT 185)

The Butterfly Tattoo is, arguably, Pullman's best novel. It deals directly with the problem of tragedy, laying open the complex forces that lead to human suffering. Love is not strong enough to defeat evil, nor is wisdom sufficiently efficacious to avert tragedy. Pullman builds a deeply ambiguous moral world around his hero, and leaves the reader to contemplate whether experience really is preferable to innocence.

In the trilogy, Pullman tries to create the same atmosphere of moral complexity, but the world of *His Dark Materials* contains very little moral ambiguity. Lyra is given a truth-telling device, the alethiometer, which means that she never has to make proper ethical choices. Lyra says, quoting Keats, that she reads the alethiometer by using 'negative capability'. Keats describes negative capability as the state when we are 'capable of being in uncertainties, mysteries, doubts, without any irritable reaching after fact and reason'.[21] In truth though, Lyra never has to employ the 'negative capability'. Her moral universe never requires her to live with uncertainty: her choices are always made clear to her.

For real people living in the real world the future is unknown and all human choices must be made in the face of this ignorance. In *The Butterfly Tattoo*, Chris Marshall must decide how to act not knowing what will happen, and his decision turns out to be wrong. But Lyra always makes the right choice based upon certain knowledge about how things will turn out. So there are no proper moral dilemmas for Lyra.

Even when she is deprived of her alethiometer, Pullman removes any moral ambiguity from Lyra's decisions. Consider the moment when Lyra must decide whether to enter the land of the dead. She describes her choice in this way: '...the angel *commanded* me. That's why we came here . . . We *got* to' (AS 282 – Pullman's italics). The decision to sacrifice herself and enter the land of the dead requires *courage*, but Lyra is never in any doubt that it is the right thing to do.

We see the same thing happening at the end of the trilogy. Lyra and Will's dæmons are sent by the angel Xaphania to explain the moral problem: it is 'vital' that someone stops Dust leaking away through the windows between the worlds, 'otherwise everything good will fade away and die' (AS 511). Lyra and Will must choose between staying together and doing their duty. Lyra is desperate and turns to the alethiometer for assistance, but the gift has left her. Just when Lyra might be facing some genuine moral ambiguity, Pullman steps in by sending the angel Xaphania in person to talk to Lyra and Will. Xaphania explains how important it is that Will and Lyra fulfil their duty. In the end, there is no moral dilemma. The correct moral choice has been spelt out by the angel (who is presumably well qualified to do such things). The only thing that Will and Lyra must decide is whether they have the courage to do what must be done. It may be a painful choice, but it contains no ambiguity.

Pullman clearly wants the world of *His Dark Materials* to be a complex moral space in which (as Mary Malone puts it) the labels 'good' and 'evil have been abolished' (AS 471). What Pullman actually creates, however, is a black and white universe with few shades of grey. Pullman projects all evil onto an abstract organisation staffed by irredeemably wicked people. All moral negativity is thus externalised. Will and Lyra do not have to work through any internal moral struggles to over-come the Authority. Their friends – Farder Coram, Serafina Pekkala, Lee Scoresby and Iorek Byrnison – are all utterly loyal. There is no Judas in *His Dark Materials* and no Peter. The spies – the Gallivespians – are paid professionals whose roles and allegiances are never in doubt. The whole story has the feeling of a tableau: the protagonists are positioned by Pullman, and hold their poses until the story is finished. The good never see their halos slip, and the bad never see the error of their ways. So there is no proper redemption in *His Dark Materials*. The good people start off good and carry on that way. The bad people are stuck with their faults.

Pullman talks ominously about betrayal in *His Dark Materials*, but it never properly happens. He says that Lyra betrays Roger because she unwittingly delivers him into the hands of Lord Asriel. This is not a betrayal, however, but a mistake. Similarly, it is prophesied that Lyra will commit a more terrible betrayal. This turns out to be the fact that she must leave behind her dæmon Pantalaimon when she visits the land of the dead. Again, this is not a betrayal in the ordinary sense of the term. Her dæmon *cannot* enter the land of the dead – it is impossible. The parting of Lyra and her dæmon involves no breach of trust or act of cruelty. In fact, their separation can only take place because of trust and loyalty.

Because Lyra is always directed towards the right choice she never has a proper moral 'experience', which would involve taking an important ethical decision with imperfect information, and reconciling conflicting beneficial ends and contradictory moral principles. In short, a moral experience would mean having to take a decision which may turn out to be wrong. Lyra never has to face this risk: the alethiometer (or visiting angels) make sure that Lyra always knows the right course of action to take.

It is not immediately obvious why Pullman controls Lyra's choices in this way. It would not be a problem from a narrative point of view to have placed Lyra in a complex ethical situation. In fact, such an episode might well have improved the novel. So why does Pullman so deliberately and consistently provide Lyra with definitive moral answers? Part of the reason is that Pullman wants to protect Lyra's innocence, to protect her from the tragedy which follows from so many human decisions. One of the influences on Pullman was an essay, 'The Marionette Theatre', by the seventeenth-century German philosopher Heinrich von Kleist. Kleist argued that adults become self-conscious and lose the easy grace of childhood. In order to recover their original naïvety, adults must learn again from experience how to be innocent. We must keep eating the forbidden fruit of experience in order to rediscover the entrance to the Garden of Eden. But Pullman never lets Lyra lose her moral innocence: she is always protected from error. Pullman does not want Lyra to taste the real fruit of experience, which is moral ambiguity, or to be mired in the messy business of human moral choices. She must remain pure and worthy of her role. Lyra must remain innocent in order to fulfil her destiny.

Lyra's alethiometer operates using Dust, and Dust is connected with the proper destiny of the human race. The alethiometer is not just telling Lyra the truth about what will happen, but is ensuring that she brings about what *ought* to happen. The novel mentions frequently the job that Lyra *must* do and the destiny that she *must* fulfil. Lyra's life is not one in which a range of choices are equally correct. If she had stayed at Jordan College this would have been 'wrong'. If she had decided that the grown-up thing was to accept Roger's death, this too would have been wrong. Lyra's moral universe does not consist of rich possibilities, but of a series of absolutely either/or right and wrong options.

Could it be, therefore, that Pullman believes in an objective moral order and that he wants the novel to communicate the belief that in every situation there is an objectively correct course of action? Could it be that Pullman is a rather old-fashioned ethicist, who believes that there is one true way to behave and that we must try to discern what this way is? If so, we may ask whether this belief in an objective moral order is really just theology by another name.

The death of God

> Ghost in tears
> O dead God
> hollow eye
> damp moustache
> single tooth
> O dead God
> O dead God
> Me
> I pursued you
> with unfathomable
> hatred

(Georges Bataille)[22]

The death of God is hardly a new idea, but Pullman tries to tell the story of God's death in a new way. Pullman shows God as 'the Authority': an impostor or a 'first angel', who after centuries of oppression and cruelty is exhausted and ready to die. When at last Will reaches the Authority, ready with his knife, the so-called Aeshetter, or god-killing knife, the weapon is not necessary. God just fades away.

The armies of God have to be fought, and Metatron (God's regent) must be defeated in hand-to-hand combat. However, God himself is not really an adversary, but a has-been: he has no power, no energy, no will to live.

His followers are all fighting to preserve their status and power. But God has no fight left in him and his death is a merciful release.

This is an original twist on the 'death of God'. Pullman is presumably saying that religious power lies with human theocracies rather than with God himself. There is no real theological power, only *theocratic* power, the power of religious organisations. If we fight against theocracies we will discover, as Will and Lyra do, that God just evaporates as if he had never existed. God is like the Wizard of Oz – small and insignificant, once his grandiose religious machinery is stripped away. And when this happens, human beings, like Dorothy and her companions, realise that their salvation lies within them.

The death of God in *His Dark Materials* is liberating, but not dangerous. Will and Lyra are liberated to fulfil their duty to ensure that Dust does not escape from the universe. They are liberated from the Authority, only to fall under the spell of a new 'authority': the absolute obligation to build the republic of heaven. But they are not liberated to moral oblivion, or confusion, or an emptiness of meaning. This is 'death-of-God-lite': God dies, but the cosmos retains all its theological meaning. Humans still have a destiny, there are still objective ethical rules and Dust still gives the universe a warm glow.

This is all very different from the death of God in, say, Nietzsche. For Nietzsche, the death of God is a massive cultural event because 'God' does not mean a divine person, but the metaphysical under-girding of all our meanings and values.

> The madman jumped into their midst and pierced them with his eyes. 'Whither is God?' he cried. 'I will tell you. *We have killed him –*

you and I. All of us are his murderers. But how did we do this? How could we drink up the sea? Who gave us the sponge to wipe away the entire horizon? What were we doing when we unchained this earth from its sun? Whither is it moving now? Whither are we moving? Away from all suns? Are we not plunging continually? Backward, sidewards, forward, in all directions? Is there still any up or down? Are we not straying as though through an infinite nothing? Do we not feel the breath of empty space? Has it not become colder? Is not night continually closing in on us?[23]

Nietzsche takes the same view as Dostoyevsky: 'if God is dead, anything is permitted'. The death of God leaves humanity without any ready-made truths or values. God used to provide all the moral rules, universal truths and systems of meaning. But when God dies, everything changes. The truth must now be *invented* and values must be *created*. Interestingly, Nietzsche says that it is generally our cultured atheists who do not realise the implications of the death of God: the madman is addressing 'those who do not believe in God'. They laugh at the madman's speech, because they think that you can kill God and leave the whole apparatus of bourgeois morality comfortably intact.

There is a rejoinder that can be offered to all who advocate the death of God: if God is dead, what is the problem? Pullman, like Nietzsche, is strangely pre-occupied with the dead God. But arguing for the death of God when you think he doesn't exist is rather like arguing for the abolition of clothes in a nudist colony. Why, if God is dead, is it necessary to destroy him?

Perhaps, in Pullman's case, it is because he would *like* God to be dead, but is *not absolutely sure* that God is?

The impulse to assert the death of God may emerge when an atheist is experiencing doubts and is concerned to confirm himself in his atheism. The death of God would provide the same kind of reassurance to an atheist as a theophany would to the believer. So we should not take Pullman's apparent enthusiasm for the death of God at its atheist face value. Lurking in Pullman's breast there is, perhaps, some religious feeling that dare not speak its name.

Heaven

> No kings, no bishops, no priests. The kingdom of heaven has been known by that name since the Authority first set himself above the rest of the angels. And we want no part of it. This world is different. We intend to be free citizens of the republic of heaven. (AS 222)

One of the big ideas in *His Dark Materials* is Pullman's suggestion that human beings should be working for something he calls 'the republic of heaven'. This is what Will and Lyra realise at the end of *The Amber Spyglass*, that they must strive to build heaven on earth. The republic of heaven is not only an idea in the world of the trilogy: Pullman has publicly advanced the idea as a personal conviction.

> I think it's time we thought about a republic of heaven instead of the kingdom of heaven. The king is dead. That's to say I believe that the king is dead. I'm an atheist. But we need heaven nonetheless, we need all the things

that heaven meant, we need joy, we need a sense of meaning and purpose in our lives, we need a connection with the universe, we need all the things that the kingdom of heaven used to promise us but failed to deliver. And, furthermore, we need it in this world where we do exist – not elsewhere, because there ain't no elsewhere.[24]

Pullman offers us what Blake called 'the Devil's account' of heaven. That Jerusalem would not be built in the sky, but 'in England's green and pleasant land'. The 'messiah' will form heaven from the materials of ordinary human experience, ordinary human work and imagination.

The republic of heaven comes about, Pullman says, when human beings apply their natural faculties and make use of the accumulation of human wisdom. But Pullman is extremely vague about how exactly we make the new republic, when it will happen and what it will look like. The republic of heaven is an article of faith in the human future: that everything will be good and bright so long as we all work together to make it happen.

Pullman assumes that the accumulation of Dust will be a good thing, that human experience will mount up providentially to create a positive human future. But Pullman does not account for human folly, error or bad intention. Dust – human experience – is simply 'benevolent' (AS 503) and 'beautiful' (AS 505). Ugly, violent or unpleasant human experiences do not seem to contribute to 'Dust', so where do they go? How is the evil and tragedy in the world to be overcome in order that we can have a good future?

The Christian myth invites individuals to live lives of sacrificial love, after the example of Jesus. The individual must make a personal change and a personal choice.

80

There must be a turning away (repentance) from an old self in order to find one's new self. These new selves are the stuff of the kingdom. And without this transformation in individual lives, nothing in human affairs can improve. This transformation is open to everyone, indeed it is particularly open to one's enemies, who must be respected and loved.

Pullman gives almost no clues about the personal transitions that must take place if the republic of heaven is to come about. Those following the Authority must, presumably, discover something about themselves or their world that persuades them to work for the new republic. But Pullman does not show us the individual processes or cultural changes that will turn history in the right direction. In general, Pullman seems to imply that the bad people must be *defeated* rather than *converted*. The new republic requires a battle in which the forces of the Authority must lose. The agents of the Authority are not turned around, but eliminated. Metatron is killed: the Authority dies; Father Gomez (Lyra's would-be assassin) is drowned in a stream.

The plot of the trilogy implies that if only we can overthrow the evil ideologies of oppression, that if only the king can be deposed from his kingdom, humanity will automatically be able to realise its mission to create heaven on earth. If only we can destroy 'them', then 'we' can get on with creating the new world order. Pullman gives us little idea of how 'they' must change, or how 'we' must grow in order to bring about the republic of heaven.

The one clue we are given to personal change is the transformation that takes place in Mrs Coulter, Pullman's most interesting character. Mrs Coulter's allegiance to the church is undermined by the maternal love that she discovers for Lyra. This love manages to break through the layers of cruelty and self-interest that make up Mrs Coulter's personality:

> I love Lyra. Where did this love come from? I don't know; it came to me like a thief in the night, and now I love her so much my heart is bursting with it . . . the love was no bigger than a mustard seed . . . the mustard seed had taken root and was growing. (AS 426–7)

Pullman must be aware of the biblical imagery here. In the Bible, the thief who comes in the night is Jesus (Matthew 24:43/Luke 12:39) and the growing mustard seed is a metaphor for faith and for the kingdom of God (Matthew 13:31 and 17:20; Mark 4:31; Luke 13:19 and 17:6). Pullman is presumably indicating that ordinary human love replaces religious faith. Religion is unnecessary because 'all you need is love'. But Pullman also raises a quasi-religious question when Mrs Coulter asks 'where did this love come from?' This is a good question and it is one that echoes in various forms through the whole of *His Dark Materials*. But look as we may in Pullman's trilogy, we will not find an answer.

In asserting the reality of a republic of heaven, Pullman takes for granted the existence of love, benevolence, destiny and providence. By contrast, the Christian myth tries to account for the existence of both goodness and tragedy in the world, and to explain how goodness can prevail against the tragic forces of destructiveness and self-interest. Pullman never offers an explanation of the victory of love. His republic of heaven depends upon the presupposition that human virtue will automatically prevail. But who, looking at human history, could hold such a naïve faith in human self-improvement? Who could believe that human beings have the degree of control over events required to make grand designs possible?

Surely Emerson was nearer the truth when he said that 'things are in the saddle and ride mankind'.

The idea that human beings can make their own perfect future is not a new idea, but one of the (now discredited) dogmas of the enlightenment. Over the past two centuries, there have been a thousand variations on the idea of republic of heaven – from Coleridge and Southey's pantisocracy to William Morris's Earthly Paradise, from socialist utopias to capitalist dreams of the 'end of history'. Without exception, human attempts to design perfect societies have failed spectacularly, and some have generated brutal tyrannies. Pullman does not give us sufficient reason to think that his republic will not fail as miserably as all the rest.

CONCLUSION

Pullman's hidden theology

> Theism and atheism are not simply . . . con-
> tradictory opinions. A bond of necessity
> stretches between them: atheism depends
> upon theism for its vocabulary, for its mean-
> ing, and for the hypotheses it rejects . . . One
> issues from the other; one cannot make sense
> unless the other does.
>
> (Michael J. Buckley, *At the Origins of Modern
> Atheism*)[1]

'Theological' questions are thrown up again and again in Pullman's writing. When he talks about 'Dust' in the trilogy, he seems to be describing some cosmic power, which is linked to human destiny and personal voca-tion. When God dies in *The Amber Spyglass* we are told that this is not really God, but a self-appointed Authority. This begs the question of what 'God' might really be. And when Pullman advocates a republic of heaven we may wonder whether this isn't just 'realised eschatology' – that's to say, the kingdom of God by another name.

Pullman's atheism is a 'theological atheism' which denies the reality of God at the same time as validating the 'theological' quest to resolve questions of 'ultimate concern': What is human nature? What is the meaning of history? What is ultimately 'real'? Pullman may kill off God in *His Dark Materials*, but he lacks the anti-theological virulence of, say, Nietzsche or Bataille. Pullman may have broken free from naïve theological realism, but he has not broken free from either the romance of theology or the theological presupposition that life does have a final meaning, purpose and reality.

What is more, everything in Pullman's counter-Christian myth has been framed by the Christian paradigm. His constellation of concepts and characters only really makes sense when referenced to Christian concepts: Dust to sin; the republic to the kingdom; Lyra to Eve; Asriel to Satan and so on. We may reasonably ask how much of the energy behind Pullman's myth really derives from the Christian myth it seeks to replace. As Nietzsche said, 'we godless anti-metaphysicians still take our fire, too, from the flame lit by a faith that is thousands of years old . . . Christian faith.'

The dilemma of atheism is that it must always be dependent upon theism. Atheism always finds itself tethered uncomfortably to the object it is trying to shrug off. When the atheist wants to say that God does not exist, he must keep asserting the identity of the God he is rejecting. What is more, the atheist is forced to make various kinds of theological counter-claim, asserting with a religious kind of faith and passion the atheist credo: that God really, truly and absolutely does not exist.

Indifference is certainly a far greater enemy to Christianity than atheism. The atheist still cares about God, even if he wants him dead. There is a kind of piety in atheism. It is this piety that keeps soaking through into the fabric of Philip Pullman's fiction. Even in his rejection of religion, in his hatred of the church and his contempt for God, Pullman is still asking theological questions and finding comfort in theological answers.

I am using 'theological' in a very general sense to mean any metaphysical understanding of 'truth': that is to say, the belief that there is an absolute truth about human life and its purpose. Theology in this 'general sense' may not speak about 'God' – indeed 'God' may have been notionally killed off – but underneath the theological denials we find a powerful system of 'theological realities': the soul, teleological purpose, personal vocation, providence and cosmic benevolence. In this 'general theological' sense we may say that Philip Pullman is an intensely religious writer.

One answer to the question of human identity is to assert the existence of an inner soul or self: Pullman does this through the dæmon. One answer to the question of the purpose of human history is to assert the reality of a good and necessary future: Pullman does this through his ideal of the republic of heaven. One answer to the question of the meaning of things is to assert some inner essence, which dwells in all life: Pullman does this through his concept of Dust. At every turn Pullman offers us religious alternatives to God.

This *religious reaction against religion* is an important phenomenon, and one which the churches should seek to understand. Pullman presents himself as an irreligious critic of Christianity, but appearances can be deceptive. Pullman's gripe with the church is that it does not respect the sanctity of life, or the human soul (dæmon). He sees the church as an instrument of authority, rather than a witness to the mysterious love that transforms even Mrs Coulter. He sees the church offering false promises of heaven, rather than motivating people to change their real social circumstances. Pullman offers a humanistic religion of life and love in place of the Christian myth of fall and redemption. We could say that Pullman's critique of Christianity amounts to the charge that its churches are *not religious enough*, that the church overlooks, or represses, or destroys the very things that religion should venerate and treasure.

Lyra, the 'new Eve', represents Pullman's new religious consciousness. Lyra is not attracted by religion or God, but by the wonder of the natural world and its variety of creatures and personalities. She is utterly loyal in her friendships with Roger, Will and Iorek Byrnison, risking her life to save or protect theirs. She is so moved by the plight of the dead that she negotiates their release from hell. And she can see the need for a universal human solidarity and is prepared to sacrifice her relationship with Will to ensure that Dust does not leak out of the universe. Lyra is motivated by curiosity, a sense of adventure and love for her friends – and is not inhibited by manners or tradition or 'authorities'. Her religion could be described as a religion of solidarity: solidarity with her inner self, with her friends and with the human race.

In many ways, Pullman's religion does not stand up to scrutiny: it fails to engage with human tragedy, for example, or the crisis of moral authority that follows from the death of God. But this is not the point. Pullman's popularity (the public chord he has struck with adults and children, ordinary readers and literary judges) tells the churches something about popular attitudes to religion. Pullman (and his readers) find Christianity life-denying and authoritarian. To them the church appears more concerned with preserving its doctrines and traditions than in celebrating the vitality and goodness of life, more concerned with power and prestige than with people and their sufferings.

The good news is that these same people appear to be attracted to a religion with humanitarian and demo-cratic values. The popularity of Pullman's trilogy does not tell us that religion is dead, but shows that many people view organised religion as ugly and restrictive. In the National Theatre production of *His Dark Materials* the church leaders were set up as pantomime villains, costumed in severe purple cassocks. The audience didn't quite boo and hiss, but they could have and it wouldn't have been out of place. But the same audience was entranced by Lyra's 'destiny' and the mystery of Dust.

If there is a lesson for the church in *His Dark Materials* it is perhaps that Christianity must offer itself to the modern world as the true religion of life and love, and rediscover its humanitarian and democratic values. This may be the time for the church to throw away its mitres, move out of its palaces and stand in more visible solidarity with the world in all its glory and suffering.

The Haunted Storm (1972)

The Haunted Storm is the story of Matthew Cortez, a nervous, conflicted young man who has a self-confessed 'God-mania' (HS 68). Matthew has clairvoyant powers and a telepathic link with his lost brother.

The novel opens in a seaside town, where Matthew is waiting and praying for something to happen, for 'a sign from God, or the Devil or any interested party' (16) and for 'emotional and sexual relief' (10). On the beach he encounters a beautiful, mysterious, androgynous woman (Elizabeth Cole). There is a 'wild and tender eroticism in the air between them' (20). She invites Matthew to touch her with one hand on condition that he does not follow her. As he masturbates her, she talks to him about her 'evil' lover and her sense of being a spirit trapped in the material world. Her lover is a satanic figure, with psycho-kinetic powers, who is determined to take away a 'Holy Well' that her father has discovered. She tells Matthew that he is the twelfth stranger she has asked to touch her, before screaming at him and running away. She regrets running away, knowing that Matthew is 'the one'.

Months have passed since the incident on the beach and Matthew goes to stay with his uncle Harry, an evangelical preacher who had 'a strange kind of moral force, as uncompromising as light' (48–9).

The visit is disturbed when an eleven-year-old girl

is murdered in the nearby woods. The following day Matthew goes to church. Matthew is captivated by the Vicar's Manichean sermon, which depicts the world as a realm of darkness and desire. This contrasts with Uncle Harry's vision of a world bathed in the love of Christ (121). The Vicar is Canon Cole, Elizabeth's father (but Matthew doesn't know this yet). Matthew asks to speak with Canon Cole to ask why God appears to be so 'dead' and 'hidden'. Then he sees Elizabeth in the churchyard. Matthew declares his love for her and sees their souls 'as one'. They resolve to have a 'puritan' relationship without sex. On a walk in town they see Elizabeth's lover and realise that it is Matthew's estranged and wayward brother Alan.

Matthew and Canon Cole discuss the nature of God. Canon Cole says that he is a Gnostic. Matthew offers Canon Cole a graphic imaginative account of the rape and murder of the young girl in the village. When asked, Matthew says that he dreamt the story. The Canon tells him about the mysterious well that he has discovered.

Matthew meets Alan and learns that he is a fascist and that he has deliberately misled people into thinking that the well is dedicated to 'the invincible god' Mithras: an excellent emblem for his new political movement, the British People's Party. The well is in fact dedicated to 'the unknown god' and represents the goal of all those searching for religious truth. Matthew worries increasingly that he is committing murders during his occasional blackouts.

Matthew, Elizabeth, Alan and the Canon go to the well during an eclipse of the moon. Matthew and the Canon end up fighting savagely. In the ensuing argument between all four of them, Alan reveals himself as the murderer and the Canon reveals that the well is really the entrance to an underground temple. Matthew

descends the steps in the well and falls into an underground river that leads to the temple. Once inside,
Matthew realises that there appears to be no way out.
Alan is able to tell Matthew telepathically that there is a
way out and that he must search for it.

Galatea (1978)

Galatea is a magical–realist novel, which explores ideas
of human reality and unreality. In particular, Pullman
poses the question of the extent to which money –
capitalism – distorts or even creates our realities.
'Galatea' is the name of an angel who forms a relationship with Martin Browning, the hero of this novel.
Browning's wife has disappeared, but he has no idea why
or where she has gone. Following a hunch he travels
south to Valencia where he meets the sinister banker
Lionel Pretorius. Pretorius helps to provide Browning
with the funds to continue his quest further south to
Venezuela. Browning travels with Pretorius' daughter
Mary, but his plans are thrown into confusion when the
plane crashes in the South American jungle. Mary
Pretorius and Browning make their way through a series
of bizarre locations: a zombie farm, and two Cities of
Unreal People. Their journey ends at the Perfect City of
Unreal People. Here Browning realises that his wife has
become part of the illusion of this perfectly unreal
world. He is helped to this understanding by Galatea
who saves Browning by sacrificing her own life. This
sacrificial love is an ultimate reality in a city where
everything else has become a commodity. Browning
returns to his own world and becomes a millionaire.
Browning's quest for the lost love of his wife is an
allegory of the struggle to know what is truly real in our
late modern capitalist society.

The Ruby in the Smoke (1985)

The first of the Sally Lockhart novels introduces Sally as a pretty, intelligent, wilful sixteen-year-old living in London in the late nineteenth century. She has been told that her mother died during the Indian Mutiny and that Captain Lockhart (the man who she thinks is her father) has recently been killed when his ship the *Lavinia* sank in the South China Sea. With the aid of a cryptic note from Captain Lockhart referring to something called The Seven Blessings, Sally sets out to find out why he died.

Sally receives a letter from Major George Marchbanks asking her to meet him about 'an item of incalculable value'. At Marchbanks' house Sally is given an important package and is warned that she is in great danger from someone called Mrs Holland who pursues her from the house. She is rescued by a photographer, Frederick Garland, who becomes her business partner and later her lover.

The package contains a manuscript by Marchbanks describing the disappearance of the Ruby of Agrapur. Sally is able to read the first page (which connects her and her father with the ruby) before it is stolen. Sally later learns that Marchbanks has been killed by Mrs Holland.

Meanwhile in Limehouse, East London, Matthew Bedwell (who is addicted to opium) is held captive by Mrs Holland who learns that he holds the key to finding the ruby. Bedwell was a friend of Sally's father and has an important message for her. Sally learns about Bedwell's condition and joins forces with his brother Nicholas (a clergyman and ex-professional boxer) to rescue Matthew from Mrs Holland's clutches. Matthew is rescued along with a girl called Adelaide. When Matthew Bedwell comes round he tells Sally that he was second mate on the *Lavinia*. The *Lavinia* was sunk by a black junk captained by Ah Ling, the most ruthless pirate in the South China Sea. Ah Ling stabbed Captain Lockhart and sank the ship to conceal his crime.

Mrs Holland thinks she has tracked the ruby down to a brass-studded box concealed behind a stone in the Turk's Head pub. But the box is empty because Jim, Sally's friend, has already taken the stone and given the ruby to Sally.

When Sally visited the opium den to release Matthew Bedwell, the smoke induced a nightmare that revealed lost memories that may be important in her quest. She decides to take some more opium (acquired to help Matthew Bedwell) to bring back the dream. The dream reveals that Major Marchbanks is Sally's true father. He sold Sally to Captain Lockhart in exchange for a ruby given to Captain Lockhart by the Maharajah of Agrapur. Mrs Holland has been blackmailing Major Marchbanks in an attempt to obtain the ruby, which she believes was promised to her by the Maharajah with whom she once had an affair.

Taking her pistol with her, Sally confronts Mrs Holland on London Bridge. Having confirmed with her the truth of her dream, Sally drops the ruby into the Thames. Mrs Holland becomes hysterical and throws herself off the bridge to her death. Sally breaks down in tears and a cab draws up beside her. A mysterious figure invites Sally to climb in. It is Ah Ling, Captain Lockhart's murderer. Ah Ling says that he killed the Captain because he interfered with the activities of his drug-dealing triad gang, The Seven Blessings. He now wants Sally to become his lover. He reaches forward with a knife, but Sally shoots him and flees from the cab. Later, the police find the cab blood-stained, but empty.

After receiving a message from Matthew Bedwell, Sally later discovers a letter from Captain Lockhart and a large sum of money to invest in a business.

The Shadow in the North / *The Shadow in the Plate* (1986)

The second Sally Lockhart novel begins with the sinking of another ship, the *Ingrid Linde*, owned by the firm Anglo-Baltic, which has now collapsed, ruining its investors. Sally had advised an elderly client to invest in Anglo-Baltic and sets out to find out what has happened to this apparently robust company. Her first lead is the involvement in Anglo-Baltic of Axel Bellman, 'the richest man in Europe' and owner of a company called North Star based in Barrow.

The lead to Bellman is echoed mysteriously by a medium called Nellie Budd who speaks about 'a shadow in the north . . . a mist full of fire – steam, and it's packed with death'. Nellie's premonition also connects with the fears of a stage magician called Alistair Mackinnon who has had a vision of a man being stabbed with a sword. Mackinnon is also apparently terrified of Bellman and Jim (one of Sally's colleagues) is warned that Mackinnon is in great danger.

Sally, who has started investigating Mr Bellman, is warned off by Mr Windlesham, Bellman's private secretary. With characteristic pluck, Sally decides to call at Bellman's offices to demand repayment of her client's losses. Bellman refuses and threatens to smear Sally as a prostitute. Later Windlesham employs a hit man, Mr Brown, to kill Sally. Mr Brown botches the job, mistakenly stabbing a woman who is staying with Sally.

Bellman is blackmailing the Cabinet minister Lord Wytham and offering to pay his debts if Wytham persuades his seventeen-year-old daughter Mary to marry Bellman. Bellman insists that Mary must be a virgin. The marriage is arranged, but there is a problem. As Frederick Garland investigates, Mackinnon's secrets slowly surface: he was Nellie Budd's lover and young Mary Wytham's husband. So Mary is not a virgin and not a spinster. Bellman knows this and this is why he is trying to kill Mackinnon.

Frederick travels to Barrow to interview a former employee of Bellman's. He learns that Bellman is constructing a 'steam gun', a terrifying train-mounted machine gun with twelve thousand barrels.

When Bellman realises how much Sally knows, he arranges for her offices to be burned down. Sally gets out alive, but Frederick (who is now her lover) is killed. With revenge on her heart, Sally travels to Barrow to find Bellman, and shoots him while he is standing in the carriage of his steam gun. The weapon explodes, destroying Bellman and his entire factory. Miraculously, Sally makes it out alive. The novel ends with the happy news that Sally is pregnant with Fred's child.

The Broken Bridge (1990)

Ginny is a happy and talented sixteen-year-old who does not know her own past. She thinks that her mother, who was a black artist, died when she was young, which is why her father, who is white, has brought her up on his own. When a social worker calls on her father one day, the threads of her true past begin to unravel.

Ginny learns that she has a half-brother (Robert) from a relationship her father had before he met her mother. Robert's mother has died and he is now coming to live with Ginny and her father. Robert and Ginny have a fierce argument in which Ginny has to listen to some home truths about her snobbish and arrogant personality.

From her friends Ginny also hears rumours that she herself is adopted, that her father has been in prison and that her mother is still alive. She tracks her mother down to a gallery in Liverpool where she is exhibiting an exciting collection of paintings about her Haitian roots. Ginny is entranced by the paintings, but her mother rejects her, saying that she only ever wanted to be an artist and not a mother. After confronting her father, Ginny learns that her mother rejected her father before she was born. Her father had to fight to get custody of Ginny, including abducting her from foster parents. As a result, her father served a prison sentence, but his paternity was officially acknowledged and Ginny came to live with him. Ginny's father also tells her about his abusive upbringing at the hands of his mother.

The Broken Bridge is a *Bildungsroman* in which Ginny comes to discover hard but important truths about herself and her past. Ginny also learns that Andy, the boy she fancies, is gay. It is also a cultural story about a black person coming to understand her heritage and place in a predominantly white Welsh community.

This novel also shows how well Pullman handles tragedy. The 'broken bridge' is the bridge back to our damaged past. As Ginny's friend Rhiannon puts it, 'It's tragic. Life's a tragedy, see' (BB 76). The bridge to Ginny's mother is broken, as is the bridge between her father and her grandparents. But if the past is tragically scarred, the future is redeemable and the novel ends on a positive note as Ginny contemplates her exciting future. The novel shows that the pain of the past must be understood. Ginny discovers that she is happier when she acknowledges and accepts her faults and shortcomings. Facing up to tragedy is the way to overcome it.

The Tiger in the Well (1991)

Ah Ling, the evil drug-dealing pirate shot by Sally at the end of *The Ruby in the Smoke*, is paralysed but very much alive, in London, and about his wicked business. He is attended to by a trained monkey, but is looking for a human child to take over when the monkey dies. Sally now has a child of just the right age.

The novel begins with Sally at the centre of a mysterious conspiracy. Legal action is being taken by a Mr Parrish who claims to be her husband and who wants custody of her child, Harriet. Sally discovers that her marriage to Parrish is legally documented and Parrish is able to take all her assets.

Sally goes on the run with her daughter. She now has to learn how to care for Harriet, having previously had others to look after her, and has to take on the day-to-day chores of motherhood. In the East End she also learns about the socio-economic predicament of her fellow Londoners, especially the plight of women in the Spitalfields Social Mission, where Sally herself finds refuge. Continuing her investigations as best she can, Sally discovers that her marriage to Parrish was forged by a vicar who is addicted to drugs.

Sally also learns about a charismatic Jewish socialist, Danny Goldberg, who has been trying to expose Ah Ling. Goldberg sends for Sally, seeing her as a possible source of information about Parrish. Goldberg is interested in Parrish because he is directly connected with Ah Ling. Sally is attracted to Goldberg because she sees him as her equal.

Ah Ling is using the name Mr Lee and has moved to a specially converted house in Spitalfields. The house has a lift to a cellar in which it is planned to imprison Harriet during her period of training to be Ah Ling's personal slave. Sally tricks her way into Ah Ling's household posing as a maid. Here she learns that Ah Ling is trying to provoke racist riots. (Goldberg is later able to subdue the rioters.) Sally also gathers evidence that proves that Parrish is involved in Ah Ling's criminal activities.

Sally manages to get into Ah Ling's bedroom and it is only now that she realises that she is confronting her old enemy. Although she has her pistol with her, she finds herself unable to shoot a defenceless and paralysed man. Ah Ling calls his servants and Sally is taken to the cellar for interrogation. Sally and Ah Ling have a long argument, which is cut short by the fact that an underground stream is sweeping away the foundations to the house. Ah Ling tells how in his native China a tiger once became trapped in a well, stopping the villagers from getting water. It was only an act of God (a downpour of rain) that drowned the tiger and saved the people. Shortly after, Ah Ling is drowned. Sally somehow manages to get herself to safety.

Sally is reunited with her daughter, her marriage is shown to be false and she decides that she will marry Danny Goldberg.

The Butterfly Tattoo / The White Mercedes (1992)

Chris Marshall is seventeen and lives in Oxford. His parents have divorced and have formed new relationships, which has left Chris displaced, isolated and in need of love. Chris works for Oxford Entertainment Systems and is installing lighting for a college summer ball. In the college grounds he meets a beautiful woman called Jenny who is running in terror from three young men. Chris protects Jenny and, in his vulnerable emotional state, becomes obsessed with her.

Jenny and Chris go out together and Chris learns that

Jenny is a drifter who is living in a squat in town. The narrator tells us that Jenny has been abused by her father. Jenny and Chris become lovers and Chris sees the butterfly tattoo on Jenny's breast. Shortly afterwards, Jenny's squat is raided for drugs and Jenny goes to stay with a friend. Jenny and Chris have not exchanged surnames, so it is impossible for them to find each other. However, by coincidence, Jenny also starts babysitting for Chris's colleague Barry Miller.

Chris has been helping Barry to wire a small shed that Barry has acquired as 'a place to go to ground' (BT 38). Barry tells Chris that he once had a 'run in' with a criminal family called Carson who were also involved with Irish terrorism. Barry says that he was working for the Secret Service in Northern Ireland and helped to get two of the Carsons convicted. He is now worried for his safety and needs the shed as a safe house. The narrator tells us that Barry's story is only half true. The Carsons were dealing in drugs and Barry had turned Queen's evidence to get Frank Carson sent down for life. Edward Carson, Frank's brother (and a very nasty piece of work) is now seeking revenge for his brother's betrayal. Edward Carson drives a white Mercedes.

After babysitting one evening, Barry tells Jenny about Carson and shows her the shed, saying that he has a plan to lure Carson there and have him arrested. He also tells Jenny that he is meeting Chris at the shed that evening. Meanwhile, Carson pays Chris a visit pretending to be Mr Fletcher, a policeman. Carson deceives Chris by telling him that Barry is a terrorist planning a vicious bombing. He persuades Chris to reveal his arrangement to meet Barry.

Later, realising his error, Chris rushes to the shed after asking a friend to phone Barry to warn him not to go there. But Barry is out and Jenny, who is babysitting, takes the call. Jenny thinks that Chris is now in danger and cycles to the shed to warn him. Carson is waiting in the darkness and shoots Jenny in error. Carson drives away in his white Mercedes.

Chris finds Jenny dead in the shed. She has written the word 'dad' in blood on the wall. Chris blames himself for Jenny's death, but realises that through these terrible events he has grown in wisdom. The novel ends very darkly with Chris (not knowing that Jenny was abused by her father) thinking that Jenny, in her dying moments, must have been calling upon her dad for help. The novel leaves the reader with complex and unanswered moral questions.

The Tin Princess (1994)

This novel is a Sally Lockhart spin-off featuring two minor characters from the earlier novels, Jim Taylor and Adelaide Bevan. Adelaide disappeared in the final scuffles with Mrs Holland and her henchmen at the end of *The Ruby in the Smoke*. Jim has been looking for her, and to his astonishment finds that she is engaged to be married to Rudolf of Eschtenburg, crown prince of Razkavia.

Adelaide is a former prostitute and commoner who must prove to the Razkavian people (and herself) that she is a worthy addition to their royal family. In the midst of the complex political struggles that make up the main plot of the book, Prince Rudolf is killed and Adelaide must become the 'eagle bearer' of Eschtenburg with responsibility for upholding its traditional values and civic order.

Northern Lights (1995)

Lyra Belacqua is twelve years old and a resident of Jordan College, Oxford in a parallel universe to our own. Lyra's world bears some resemblance to ours, but has many unusual aspects. In Lyra's world people's souls take the form of animal 'dæmons'. Until puberty dæmons can change shape, but in adulthood they become fixed. Lyra's world is dominated by a church that is obsessed with science and power. We soon learn that a department of the church, the General Oblation Board or GOB, has been abducting children. Lyra's father (Lord Asriel) and her mother (Mrs Coulter) have left her in the care of Jordan College, where she is allowed the freedom to roam half-wild around the town with her friend Roger.

Lyra overhears Lord Asriel, a scientist and explorer, talking about experiments on a substance called 'Dust'. Dust has some special significance in children and is associated with the Aurora Borealis or Northern Lights. Shortly after this, Mrs Coulter appears to take custody of Lyra. Before Lyra departs, the Master of Jordan College gives Lyra a rare truth-telling device called an alethiometer, which is all but impossible to use. But Lyra has a unique intuitive gift that allows her to read the alethiometer. We also learn that Lyra has a special 'religious' destiny.

Lyra escapes from Mrs Coulter and falls under the protection of the Gyptian boat people, who have lost children to the GOB. Lyra learns that her friend Roger has also been abducted and sets out with the Gyptians to find out what has happened. The clues lead north to Trollesund in Lapland where Lyra finds new allies: Serafina Pekkala (a witch), Iorek Byrnison (an armoured bear) and Lee Scoresby (an aviator with a hot air balloon). The trail leads to Bolvangar, an experimental station run by Mrs Coulter in the frozen wastes, where children are separated from their dæmons. Lyra is captured and taken to Bolvanger, where she finds Roger and escapes. She travels further north in Lee Scoresby's balloon, until it crashes and she falls into the hands of the rogue king of the armoured bears, Iofur Raknison. Iorek is their true king and, after some scheming by Lyra, Iorek defeats Iofur in single combat.

Now Lyra is able to make the last stage of her journey to discover what Lord Asriel is doing. When she reaches Asriel's laboratory she realises that he is planning something horrific. In order to break through the Aurora to another world, Lord Asriel needs the energy that is released when a child is separated from its dæmon. Lord Asriel is on a mission to destroy the Authority and end the power of the church. Asriel uses Roger, ruthlessly killing him in order to travel into a parallel universe. Lyra commits herself to a new quest: to find out more about the substance 'Dust' that held such importance for Asriel. So she and her dæmon follow Asriel through a rupture in the Aurora.

The Subtle Knife (1997)

Lyra finds herself in a strange world, Cittàgazze, where there are no adults. Here she meets Will Parry, a boy from our universe, who is on the run from the police and who has found a window into Cittàgazze, a parallel world to our own. Will's father is an adventurer called John Parry, an ex-Royal Marine who mysteriously disappeared on an expedition. Will's mother is mentally ill and Will has to care for her. Will's mother is interviewed repeatedly by mysterious and threatening officials wanting to know where Will's father has gone. Will has decided to leave home, when the officials break into his house. In his dash to escape, Will pushes one man downstairs and kills him. Will has no choice but to flee.

Just as Lyra obtains her alethiometer, Will takes possession of a magical knife after fighting a young man called Tullio and killing him. Will has two fingers severed in the fight and the wound refuses to heal. The knife can cut windows between worlds. The church has an agent in Will's world: Sir Charles Latrom (Lord Boreal in Lyra's world), who is determined to get his hands on the knife. He steals Lyra's alethiometer as bait, but Will is able to cut a window into Sir Charles' study to retrieve the alethiometer.

In Will's world, Lyra meets a scientist called Mary Malone who is experimenting with 'dark matter'. It appears that dark matter and Dust are related. Mary's association with Will and Lyra puts her in danger and, after receiving instructions from angels on her computer, she also leaves her world. Mary has no idea where her new journey will take her and we do not find out until *The Amber Spyglass*.

Lee Scoresby is on his own search to find Dr Stanislaus Grumman, also known as John Parry (Will's father) and 'Jopari'. On his way, Scoresby kills an agent of the church, but not before the agent has notified the Magisterium. Scoresby finds Grumman in a remote tribal village. Grumman explains that he is a shaman who has mystically summoned Scoresby so that Scoresby's balloon can take them to the bearer of the subtle knife. (Grumman does not yet know that the knife bearer is his son.) Grumman and Scoresby travel to meet Will, fighting off the church's fleet of zeppelins and continuing on foot. Scoresby is killed in the ensuing fire-fight.

Lord Asriel is gathering forces to fight the Authority and the armies of the church are also assembling in vast numbers. Other independent groups, like the witches and the angels, are taking Asriel's side.

Meanwhile, the witches are also looking for Lyra and arrive just in time to get Will and Lyra out of danger from the children of Cittàgazze who want to avenge Tullio's death. The witches try unsuccessfully to heal Will's injured hand with a spell. When Will stumbles upon his father (Grumman), he is able to heal Will's wound. Grumman tells Will that he must take the knife to Asriel who needs it to defeat the Authority. No sooner have they met than Grumman is tragically killed by Juta Kamainen, a witch whose advances Grumman has rejected.

Will says that he will find Asriel, as his father has instructed. Two angels appear saying that they have been charged to look after Will. Will goes to find Lyra, but she has been abducted, leaving her alethiometer behind.

The Amber Spyglass (2000)

Lyra has been captured and kept sedated by Mrs Coulter, who is realising her maternal love for her daughter and now trying to protect her from the church. Will is helped by angels (Baruch and Balthamos) to find Lyra and rescue her. Although Will breaks his knife in the rescue, Iorek Byrnison is able to mend it.

Mary Malone finds herself in the land of the Mulefa, curious wheeled elephants whose existence is threatened by a change in the flow of Dust. Using her scientific skills, Mary is able to save the Mulefa.

Gallivespian spies – minute people from another world – join Lyra and Will and the angels as they travel to the land of the dead to rescue Roger from his imprisonment there by the Authority. In order to enter the land of the dead, Lyra and Will must be parted from their dæmons.

Meanwhile the church is plotting against Lyra, sending an assassin after her (Father Gomez) and trying to kill her with a devious 'anbaric' bomb that can detect individual targets over vast distances. Mrs Coulter joins forces with Lord Asriel and acts as his spy in the church headquarters in Geneva.

In the land of the dead, Lyra finds Roger and Will finds his father. They both realise that their mission is to release all the souls of the damned from their torment by the Authority. Lyra uses her story-telling skills to persuade the harpies guarding the dead to show them the exit from the land of the dead. The dead souls disperse blissfully into the cosmos.

Emerging from the land of the dead, Lyra and Will find themselves in the midst of the battle between the forces of the Authority and Asriel's rebel army. Asriel and Mrs Coulter destroy Metatron (the Authority's regent) and Will and Lyra watch the powerless Authority blow away in the wind.

Mary Malone is reunited with the children and is able to tell them about her disillusionment with religion and a past love affair. Lyra and Will begin to realise their mutual love and sexual attraction.

The angel Xaphania finds the children's dæmons and leads them back to Will and Lyra. The dæmons and Xaphania explain the complicated reasons why Will and Lyra must separate in order to stop Dust flowing away. They separate and Lyra realises that she must now strive to fulfil Lord Asriel's dream of a republic of heaven.

SELECT BIBLIOGRAPHY

Amato, Joseph, *Dust: A History of the Small and the Invisible* (University of California Press, 2000).

Ballard, J. G., *Crash* (Vintage, 1995).

Buckley, Michael J., *At the Origins of Modern Atheism* (Yale University Press, 1987).

Calvino, Italo, *Invisible Cities* (Picador, 1979).

Cupitt, Don, *The Meaning of It All in Everyday Speech* (SCM, 1999).

— 'Art and Sacrilege' (unpublished essay).

Eckhart, Meister, *Works*, tr. C. B. Evans (London, 1924).

Empson, William, *Milton's God* (Chatto and Windus, 1961).

Hunt, Peter and Lenz, Millicent, *Alternative Worlds in Fantasy Fiction* (Continuum, 2001).

Nietzsche, Friedrich, *The Gay Science*, tr. W. Kaufmann (Vintage, 1984).

Ogden, J. Gordon, *The Kingdom of Dust* (Popular Mechanics Company, 1912).

Plato, *The Phaedrus* (Penguin, 1973).

Plato, *The Symposium* (Penguin, 1951).

Rustin, M. and M., 'A new kind of friendship', *Journal of Child Psychotherapy*, vol. 29, no. 2, 2003.

— 'Learning to say goodbye', *Journal of Child Psychotherapy*, vol. 29, no. 3, 2003.

— 'Where is home?', *Journal of Child Psychotherapy*, vol. 29, no.1, 2003.

Squires, Claire, *His Dark Materials Trilogy: A Reader's Guide* (Continuum, 2003).

Tucker, Nicholas, *Darkness Visible: Inside the World of Philip Pullman* (Wizard Books, 2003).

Williams, Rowan, *Lost Icons: Reflections on Cultural Bereavement* (T & T Clark, 2000).

Winnicott, D. W., *The Child, the Family and the Outside World* (Penguin, 1964).
— 'Transitional objects and transitional phenomena', *International Journal of Psychoanalysis*, 34 (1953).

NOTES

Part One: Introduction

1 'A tale which holdeth children from play', interview with Philip Pullman, *Interzone,* 161, November 2000.
2 Antonia Fraser, cover endorsement to the 1972 edition.
3 Andrew Marr, *Daily Telegraph,* 24 January 2004.

Part Two: The Story-teller

1 'Author Pullman finds it impossible to believe', interview with Philip Pullman by Heather Lee Schroeder, *Capital Times,* October 2000. *Capital Times* online: www.madison.com
2 'Heat and Dust', interview with Philip Pullman by Huw Spanner, *Third Way,* 2000. www.thirdway.org.uk
3 'Author Pullman finds it impossible to believe', Schroeder, *Capital Times.*
4 Quoted in 'Author puts Bible Belt to the test', the *Observer,* 26 August 2001.
5 'Art and Sacrilege', Don Cupitt, unpublished essay.
6 *What Does the Bible Say About the Pullman Trilogy?,* Scripture Union Connect Bible Study, p. 3.
7 'Author Pullman finds it impossible to believe', Schroeder, *Capital Times.*
8 kidsreads.com, interview, 12 December 2001; 'Voluntary Service', *Guardian,* December 2002.
9 'Faith and Fantasy', *Encounter* radio discussion, March 2002.
10 Philip Pullman, interviewed by Susan Roberts for Christian Aid, 2000.
11 'Heat and Dust', Spanner, *Third Way.*
12 *New Humanist,* vol. 117, issue 1, March 2002.
13 Philip Pullman interview for *Locus,* 479, December 2000.
14 'Heat and Dust', Spanner, *Third Way.*

15 *New Humanist*, vol. 117.
16 'A tale which holdeth children from play', interview with Philip Pullman, *Interzone*, 161, November 2000.
17 Italo Calvino, *Invisible Cities* (Picador, 1979), p. 104.
18 J. G. Ballard, *Crash* (Vintage, 1995).
19 Random House website Question and Answer with Philip Pullman.
20 'Faith and Fantasy', *Encounter* radio discussion, March 2002.
21 *Guardian*, December 2003.
22 'Pullman lays down moral challenge for writers', *Guardian*, August 2002.

Part Three: Themes and Issues

1 Philip Pullman, Tomora Piecre and Christopher Paolini in discussion on powells.com, July 2003.
2 Cited in Isaiah Berlin, *Freedom and its Betrayal* (Pimlico, 2003), pp. 148–9.
3 Philip Pullman interviewed by Susan Roberts for Christian Aid, 2000.
4 Ibid.
5 Kirk and Raven, *The Presocratic Philosophers* (CUP, 1960), p. 213.
6 Plato, *Apology,* 31d and 40b.
7 Plato, *Symposium*, 202e–203a.
8 'Author Pullman finds it impossible to believe', interview with Philip Pullman by Heather Lee Schroeder, *Capital Times*, October 2000. *Capital Times* online: www.madison.com.
9 See for example, M. and M. Rustin, 'A new kind of friendship', *Journal of Child Psychotherapy*, vol. 29, no. 2, 2003.
10 Rowan Williams, *Lost Icons* (T. & T. Clark, 2000), p. 27.
11 D. W. Winnicott, 'Transitional objects and transitional phenomena', *International Journal of Psychoanalysis*, 34, 1953.
12 Don Cupitt, *The Meaning of It All in Everyday Speech* (SCM, 1999).
13 Meister Eckhart, *Works*, tr. C. B. Evans (London, 1924).
14 J. Gordon Ogden, *The Kingdom of Dust* (Popular Mechanics Company, 1912).
15 Shakespeare, *Cymbeline*, act IV, scene ii.

16 Joni Mitchell, 'Woodstock', *Ladies of the Canyon* (Reprise, 1970).
17 C. S. Lewis, *The Magician's Nephew* (Grafton, 2002), p. 25.
18 G. W. F. Hegel, *Lectures on the Philosophy of Religion* (University of California Press, 1988), p. 284.
19 John Milton, *Paradise Lost,* Book VIII.
20 John Milton, *Paradise Lost*, Book VIII, Lines 614–628.
21 Letter to George and Thomas Keats, December 1817.
22 Georges Bataille, *Complete Works* V, p. 121.
23 Friedrich Nietzsche, *The Gay Science*, § 125.
24 'The Republic of Heaven', *Horn Book Magazine*, vol. LXXVII, No. 6, 2001.

Conclusion

1 Michael J. Buckley, *At the Origins of Modern Atheism* (Yale, 1987), p. 15.

INDEX